Twelve Words for Moss

ELIZABETH-JANE BURNETT

Twelve Words for Moss

ALLEN LANE
an imprint of
PENGUIN BOOKS

ALLEN LANE

UK | USA | Canada | Ireland | Australia
India | New Zealand | South Africa

Allen Lane is part of the Penguin Random House group of companies
whose addresses can be found at global.penguinrandomhouse.com

Penguin
Random House
UK

First published 2023
001

Set in 10.2/14.25pt Sabon LT Pro
Typeset by Jouve (UK), Milton Keynes
Printed and bound in Great Britain by Clays Ltd, Elcograf S.p.A.

The authorized representative in the EEA is Penguin Random House Ireland,
Morrison Chambers, 32 Nassau Street, Dublin D02 YH68

A CIP catalogue record for this book is available from the British Library

ISBN: 978-0-241-55683-2

www.greenpenguin.co.uk

Contents

'*Let us sing more cheerful songs*'
Friedrich Schiller, Ode to Joy

I. GLOWFLAKE

The air forgets its melody. Cloud moves fast over moon – wind-whipped, starless, un-tuned. I curl up in the mosses as wind bashes into bark, grass, heart – gusts around the parts that we forget to fill. And it is so convincing, this battering, that we forget that there was ever anything else. We forget that there are stars. We forget luminosity. We forget that a body could be for more than weathering.

Though the one I loved has gone, there are echoes. Reverberations that stay, as a note throbs after it's sounded. There are gestures, little mirrors, in people I pass, in clouds, in grass. Little tremors of what he is now, without a body. At first, I watch secretly. I do not want sadness to see. I want it to believe it still has all of me. But, as body brushes field – the ground we shared while he lived – there is a release. Even in ice there is potential to crease. Even in wind, the rumour of wings.

From the mosses' cushion, I watch my father's absence bob over like a bubble. I bounce him from knee to knee and think – what if everyone else on the earth has their own lost thing, bouncing in a bubble above them? I begin to picture us passing our losses amongst ourselves, playing a gentle, disembodied catch. So that we come to share in this loss that is at once personal and collective, completely our own and yet universal. Not a single moss but a colony. Not a single loss but a litany. Perhaps, then, there could be an ease, even in terror, when you start to feel part of something wider, when you breathe in different places. When the corner is breathing. When in front of is breathing. When behind you is breathing. It is such a relief to let go of yourself and to still be there. Or to get inside that terror, wholly inside, and to still see something out of the corner of your eye that saves you, that grounds you, that says it will be there when you climb out.

Sadness will want to keep this from you. By saying your

experience is unique and too unsettling to share, it will strip all temperance from the air. It will trust that when the trees are a dark mass and the hills lost to the blackening, at the first shining you will be undone. Sadness is so utterly silver in tongue. It will declare itself an ally, then deny that it lied if you do ever start to see light. In the darkness, it will tell you it is all that exists, in the light it will tell you, you cannot trust it. If you aren't used to luminescence, it will be easy to be fooled – it is always so much easier to believe the bad than good.

But as I lie, bobbing on the knee of the earth, keeping upright only for as long as one life takes, the lost things of those around me are bouncing too – falling and landing, landing and falling. Some moss cells are made empty, so they can fill with water. Could I have been made empty, so as to fill with light? This close to the ground, I can keep such hopes hidden. I don't need to let on that I know it is wrong to go about loss separately, when it is nothing that is not felt by every other pulsing thing, when it is nothing that the earth doesn't already know, with cycles of it everywhere.

Breathing in the boundary layer, I assume a moss' position. In being the first to come where nothing grew before, is moss. In having cells that are dead but keeping them with you anyway, is moss. In the rush of green as new life sheens. In holding a space for emptiness. In trying again. In extending. In allowing new parts of yourself to grow. In tending. In knowing that death is not an ending. In carrying a microscopic joy inside that builds until it is your strongest guide. And so, I follow its course through heather and gorse, through valley and wood and marsh and fen where it says with such force that we can start again – not without what is lost but with it kept close – the earth carries all kinds of ghosts.

SCANNICLIFT

At the first valley floor lined with oak, my hand comes to rest on the rope circling the gatepost. There are twines that hold a border in place across time, thousands of hands touching them over hundreds of years: little loving links across the landscape. I let my fingers pause and soak in the centuries. When I lift the thread and scale the hill, I reach a low bough strewn with thick mosses. In these short, crisp days, it can be hard to find the light but their shining bodies show how not to lose sight of what's already here, though indistinct – the light is so much closer than we think. In the northern hemisphere, the earth is nearest to the sun around the winter solstice. Mosses gleam like dwarf stars from the oak's surface.

In this small Teign valley woodland, layer upon layer of life is thatched and settled in. I stroke their rise and fall over wood. Part of me yearns to pick them, to let my fingers sink and scoop up the softness. Perhaps I could line my pockets, or jacket, like sheepskin, or moss-skin. Or perhaps I could slip them into my shoes and so have a part of this place always with me, as I walk through tight streets and small rooms back in Birmingham. Though I can't bring myself to disturb these living bodies, it requires a huge wrench to move away.

Further in, more deep mosses spill over rocks in a loose circle. Could I pick these? They don't seem so wedded to rock as the others did to wood. A nip here, a tug there – it could be easily done – but I pull myself away, coming over the top of the precipice. Here is a cave I remember, surrounded by large boulders tapering off in size to smaller ones that lean against fallen logs. I am approaching a part of the copse I call Cave Valley. Now managed by the Devon Wildlife Trust, this used to be a working woodland. The quarry caves are reminders of its mining history and how my relatives, centuries ago, used to run manganese workings nearby. The empty cave mouths widen, the further in I go.

Darkness lifts. Here, encircled in green: the first deep shift. There is a conjuring act, with moss, that lets me slip between time and space. In these moments, it is as though the present empties and the body readies to receive whatever comes in its place.

GLOWFLAKE

Thuidium tamariscinum, Common Tamarisk-moss

Oh love, oh leaping heart, oh stag! Oh Pythagoras! Oh to believe your light is my light, as if you weren't lit without me. Oh hoof! Oh bicycle! Oh bell! Oh travelling sailor, flung from one port to another. Oh drop! Oh rain! Oh wellington boot on fennel, puddle, pedal, across terrain. Oh to be four again! Imagine living next to somebody every day and to actively like them and yet not know them so that when they arrive at your door fully grown and more intimate than a bone, is it politeness you practise or do you run, ecstatic through your repertoire of dances? Oh furry antler branches! Come in!

Let me only now begin. To respond to the thing we named you. Common? Oh musical box! Oh foxglove! Oh elfin chicken wire! Oh downy choir! Oh quiet symphony. Living with you is a luxury. Oh sugar mouse. Oh leafy flounce. Oh forest fleece, I apologize for the breach in naming. So let us begin again, old friend. Please. Let me use my words that only come out at parties. Hummingbird. Hawk-moth. Hill-fluff. Hedge-heart. Oh flickering filament. Oh chlorophylled cinnamon, speckled shaman of the grass. I haven't come close. I don't like to impose. The lens is still in its case, oh heathery lace, oh field charm, oh Glowflake, oh lemon face! Shall we go now, to the place you always take me? To the soft quilt of ferny lilt, the place your name always conjures.

I continue along the rock floor, edging closer to the cave, slowly building up a picture of its residents. I do not let my brain take short-cuts. From green, to moss, to leaf, to branch, to stem, to rhizoid, to teeth, to hair, to cell. Here and there, a memory. Here and there, a feeling erupting, little surges of connection, as I recognize those already familiar and come to greet those that are new.

I am eager to reach the cave wall. This rock would have been here when my ancestors were – when my grandfathers, several times removed, were involved in the mining – when the caves first came into being. As I move through the copse, I think of the men's hands on this rock, on twine, on moss. I learn these men's names, as I learn the mosses'.

Samuel Archer, my fifth great-grandfather, had bought a neighbouring farm – where I have walked over from today – in the early nineteenth century, from the profits of the mining. His was a new way of working with the land and a diversion from the farming practices of his predecessors. While many may feel an attachment to rock, as to soil, with particular tones and textures reflecting specific localities and homes, for others, it lacks the animism of plants, who may, in turn, lack the consciousness of animals. Within such a hierarchy of empathy, the act of hacking into rock may fall beneath the felling of trees, or slaughter of animals, and, yet, I do not wish to tear this rock from this earth, as I do not wish to tear the moss from the rock. Still, moving through the moss-freckled basalt, I think again how much I should like to have a piece of this moss with me, or to carry one hardened flame of earth away.

I run through the scale of the extraction, from small to large, as though from one musical note to another – the removal of a stone or a stem, to the mining of manganese during the Industrial Revolution in this valley, to the large-scale operations of global mining conglomerates today, then back down again. Did that time, when Samuel drilled here, mark the beginning of the era many think of as the Anthropocene? Or was it later, with the detonation of the first atomic bomb, a hundred years after his death, or earlier, thousands of years before his birth, at the start of the Agricultural Revolution?

The ancestors of these mosses may have been here with Samuel. Known as a pioneer species, one of the first to colonize an area that may have not known, or been hospitable to life, mosses can grow without soil. They can even help to create it. On unexposed rock, in the crevices, moss can take hold. Crouched low, I circle their bodies' orbs. Might there be a way to start again, to take a very small thing and edge it into what is barren, as a spore might, like a chain of cells' lights? Often, groups of mosses persist in the same area, as with people. There is now only one known part of my family in this area, still farming. A couple of valleys away, I can't make them out through the mosses, trees, hedges, hills. But, as they tread upon on the earth, as I tread upon the earth, there is a low tremor – not of jungle drums but forest hum. We would not recognize each other if our faces met, yet, perhaps there might still be trace elements that connect.

Darkness lifts. By a profusion of *Polytrichum commune*, Common Haircap, I think of its changeling nature under a microscope – how it is one thing in the light and another in the lens. In the daylight: a clump of green, with rough stalks. An interesting shape, spikily sculptural but not extraordinary. Under the lens, it is on fire. Covered in glitter. Embers spark and scatter across its metamorphosing form.

And it is like that, too, with people. One thing in the daylight, in the routine pattern of ourselves but quite another in the moments when the habitual slips and the light shifts. In these times we are revealed, to ourselves as much as to others. It is then that we spark and scatter across our metamorphosing form. It is then that there is recognition and a sense of coming home.

CAVE VALLEY

I take shelter in a dome of birch but the rain deepens, forcing me back. I nudge under the outstretched bough of an ancient oak – its mossy covering flows, fluid like a majestic sea serpent. Once more, I feel a sudden shift. As the mosses soak up rain, they fill with green, like a light coming on. There is a charge, channelling through the leaves, similar to what is perceived under a microscope. Making slides with Sphagnum stem leaves, I have felt the same sudden takeover. Branched. Sparkling eaves of green wheat. Tiny tips of treasure, retrieved.

A compound microscope can take you even closer. Seen under its lens, a moss leaf becomes an ethereal, underwater creature, with the long writhe of itself channelling endlessly, rhythmically, luminous. While most of the other plants show intricacy of colour, tone and shape, the Sphagnum is elegantly simple. Its cells are blank – just spaces for water to fill.

LITTLE LOSS

Sphagnum girgensohnii, Girgensohn's Bog-moss

You are mostly dead. Your colourless hyaline cells fringed
by little specks of the living – small cholorophyllose cells, linked
through your leaves like chainmail. Death, bordered by life; death
bordered by life; repeating relentlessly through the body.

And we do hold dead things inside us. Things we have lost:
people, objects; dreams that never crossed into life, or saw enough
light, get carried in us everywhere we go. But your dead hyaline
cells retain the water your pores let in and out. They enable you to
access your environment. They are not redundant.

So when we are told to 'move on' from loss; I do not really
understand it. If we carry our losses in us, they can be spaces that
link us to the places we are in. They can be conduits for things that
flow to move through us: thought, warmth, laughter, song. We
cannot stagnate where death is an opening.

Nestled in a crack in the Cave Valley rock-face, the rock above meets exactly the top of my head, so that, standing up straight, I seem to slot in perfectly. I have returned to this place that I shared with my father, that our ancestors passed between them like a handshake, wondering if any part of him remains. Sun flicks through. The rock above my head, touching my hair, gives a gentle pressure. I think of all the times my father held me in his hands. Particular moments. When I drove a garden fork through my foot in the garden. When I trapped my foot in a bed sheet and imagined I was paralysed. When he threw me up so high in the air that I could touch the ceiling. When he shook my hand when I got into university. When I held his, in the hospital. Such a small gesture, this taking something in your hands. Not as large as an embrace, or total as a kiss, it is just a shape that says: here is a space I have made for you: come in. Here is a space that will welcome you in.

I open my eyes, which are streaming, to the green of the moss teeming with water and sun caught like mortar between rocks. A glow spreads from the moss at my feet to the sunlight overhead; around each dead cell, a lightness spreads. As my attention is drawn upwards, I become aware of myself as a small figure in a rock crevice in a valley in the side of a hill amid other hills, tiny, as microscopic as any moss. And I ask myself how I should like to be treated, were someone to approach me, as I approach that moss. I find that I am not that concerned with being identified but that I would rather like to be touched. To feel the small grace of a palm.

As the rain shatters down so hard that I have to leave, I trail my hand through the mosses. I want to keep the motion light, but it is hard to keep moving – each moss draws me in and keeps me close. My hand lingers on a cluster of *Rhytidiadelphus loreus*, I feel it swirl and bend beneath me, then, unexpectedly, a warmth. I move my hand to a clump of *Thuidium tamariscinum* (Glowflake). A heat here, too, but different. This is all-over, building, like feeling an iron come on. I move back to the *Rhytidiadelphus*: heat, but in spasms. Little pin-pricks of electricity.

When I say goodbye, for the thousandth time, to my father, I find myself asking him what matters. What, if he was here, would he say was important? I tell him that I am going now, to see my mother, and it is then that I feel his reply. Something about the need to love well. Something about keeping those you love close by. *Yours was a great love!* I find that I have said this out loud. *Yours was a great love!* are the only words to have entered the rock-space and I am glad of it. And though there can be a great effort in the contact of people, there can also be a radiation, I know, as I wade back through the mosses to a human world, to a particular love.

Darkness lifts, as I think of the first mosses to grow here. How a small spore of soil may have blown over and caught in the moss fronds. How invertebrates followed. How some mosses died, creating humus, providing a substrate for vascular plants. And how emptiness needn't last. Where nothing has risen, one touch can ignite in the dark. Where nothing is living, moss can be the spark that triggers new life.

2. FLAMAMBULIST

BIRMINGHAM

Moss can be the spark that triggers new life, waking what sleeps in the core of the night. Something moves in the sediment. I see through to the edge of it. Remembering what we were before we became, highlights the falseness of every new frame: sadness knows only a partial gaze, cannot see how we were built to blaze. Millions of years ago, when plants first moved from water onto land, mosses were at the forefront of how to adapt. Special tissues lessened the impact of ultraviolet light and heat. In a hot, bright world outside the water, mosses showed how to move forward.

In the path to Alys' allotment, between cracks in tarmac, *Ceratodon purpureus*, Redshank – also known as Fire Moss, burns. One of the hardiest of the pioneering moss species, it can tolerate more pollution in the air and ground than most, so is a frequent urban dweller, managing to carve a life from the dirtiest over-trodden pavement or path. On this hot day – extraordinarily so for February – in the shaded parts of the path, the moss is rather a dull brown, stubbly with drought. While weather reports bleat about sun and ice-cream, we feel a deep uneasiness, taking off our outer layers uncomfortably, like the stringy skins of bananas not quite ready to come off.

In *Hidden Nature*, Alys' book exploring plants along Birmingham's canals, she describes how she 'started noticing mosses everywhere'. She had found herself at a point in her life where she was 'back to looking at my feet, back to homing in on detail to block out the larger picture'.[1] Similarly, mosses make a good first port of call after grief. As the eyes are beginning to refocus, after the large flare of its blinding glare, it can help to locate something small – it can help to have something nearby on which to call. Since the pioneering mosses don't only seek wide open spaces or 'virgin' territories but may make homes in the well-worn, nondescript places others overlook, they can often be found close by – overhead on a rooftop, or pressed underfoot.

Increasingly, as I follow the mosses, I find myself drawn to the women who notice them too, who live and work with them in all kinds of habitats. I have started to picture these pioneers of noticing as a group all of their own: the 'women in the wetlands'. No strangers to mosses' properties, indigenous women in north-west America knew they could be used to make babies' nappies and provide sanitary protection long before these qualities were recorded by male ethnographers, as contemporary pioneer Robin Wall Kimmerer describes in *Gathering Moss: A Natural and Cultural History of Mosses*. Nineteenth-century-American Elizabeth Britton was the inspiration behind the female bryologist in Elizabeth Gilbert's novel *The Signature of All Things*, while, in the UK, Eleonora Armitage was a founding member of the Moss Exchange Club in 1896 – the oldest bryological society in the world (later becoming the British Bryological Society). Alys, a further pioneer, is just a short hop across the city from me.

She tips the watering can, head bent, her sleek red hair glowing over the dry moss. As we move up and down her path, dousing it with water, I am conscious that it is a stretch to think of this urban allotment as a wetland. But there are journeys to come, though I don't know it now. Crouched low over the path that we have made a river, I don't yet know that there will be Sphagnum pools, slippery as soup to ease into, that there will be ice-cold waters netted with mosses to curl up in like a fish, that there will be stretches of bog and moss and myrtle that will blast through the head like an arctic wind. All I know is that there is something near me I hadn't appreciated before, that there is life I could never have imagined in store.

Alys makes a small fire to boil water for tea before finishing watering the moss, which had been too dry, at first, for us to see properly.

'By the time we've had a cup of tea, it should be looking better.' I find that Alys always has a plan. While watering the moss, the tea is brewing; while drinking the tea, the moss is stewing. There is a design and economy in her movements, while I am amorphous, spreading like mist over any horizon. And that has its benefits. I can soak up, like the moss, much of my surroundings. But, similarly, I can find myself static when I should be moving. It can be up to other bodies to pick me up on the back of their shoes and lift me over to a new patch of my life.

Alys' campfire lights a memory of Embu, in Kenya, and the embers my relatives would gather around as bananas baked. My mother's side of the family had settled in the foothills of Mount Kenya and I had visited their home as a child. On these visits there had been an entirely different set of flora to contend with from those I had grown up with in my own stretch of Devon countryside.

'What's this?' I would ask, carefully noting down the name of each new plant, occasionally plucking pieces to place in my pocket. They had called me the 'Doctor' because of this habit of picking plants to make potions. I run my fingers through my pocket now. It contains a shred of Fire Moss Alys gave me a moment ago, a piece of *Brachythecium rutabulum* from my own Birmingham garden, and an empty packet, awaiting future inhabitants.

In Kenya, asking for the names of plants had been no easy business. The answers would come first in Kikuyu, or Kiyembu – local dialects. Then, after some conferring, a Swahili equivalent would be suggested. English would be the last stop on this naming journey, provided either by a cousin or my mother. I was often drawn to the Kikuyu words, although I didn't find them easy to remember. I suddenly wanted very badly to wander around those plants, muttering those Kikuyu words, committing them to memory, as I had done with the Latin names for mosses.

In the Linnaean naming of plants, a binomial name is given to the plant in Latin – first its genus, then its species. The same is true for animals, so that humans have the name *Homo sapiens*. There is a sense of objectivity that comes from using Latin that takes precedence over the common names in other languages that may prove more unreliable in their multiplicity. In the Linnaean system, every identified living species is also placed in a hierarchy that stretches from phylum at the top, down through class, order, family and genus.

A taxonomist wishing to name a group of organisms needs to assign that group a rank, such as genus or family, but as more and more complex branching is being discovered, existing ranks are proving insufficient. Even the Latin names for mosses, as Ron Porley and Nick Hodgetts suggest in their foreword to *Mosses and Liverworts*, 'are not immutable' with 'many recent changes in nomenclature'.[2] Most English common names for mosses have only been invented recently and not all mosses have them. Perhaps, in this climate of new naming, there is an opportunity to do things differently.

FLAMAMBULIST

Ceratodon purpureus, Redshank (Fire Moss)

If flames were pillows and heat was silk, if burning billowed and
scars were milk, if flesh was leaf and tear was tender, if feet were
clouds and air an ember – you could be walking through fire; you
may know moss as a pyre without harm, a movement charm,
monitoring without thought of capture, safeguarding, the only
fracture coming from your letting go of what's no longer needed,
so as to rise more deftly, so as to fall correctly.

When I had asked Mum for the Kikuyu word for moss, she said she didn't think there was one – nor in Swahili either.

'Perhaps it's too dry for moss there,' she had wondered.

'What about the rainy season?' I asked. I soon learned that there were hundreds of known moss species in Kenya and a number that grew around her old home. I wondered how mosses might enter the language of that place and asked her how to say: *a group of small plants growing together*. At first she said she didn't know – it took a while to stir the embers. Then she caught one word: *'ishi'* ('living', or 'growing'). 'That's come from the back of the head,' she had said, like a hound catching hold of the scent. She attached it to the prefix *'wana'* to form *'wanaishi'* and from this, the full phrase grew: *'makundi kindogo ya mmea kumea wanaishi pamoja'*.

Back on Alys' allotment path, the water begins to take hold. The Fire Moss spreads its large veins out as spots come to life on the path – little limelights in the dark. Alys strides over and gestures me across.

'Look,' she says, and it is like following the landing lights at an airport, mossy indicators shining all the way along the centre. We get down close, on our knees, straining over stalks with hand lenses. There are some fruiting bodies that we crane ever closer to, as Alys' clear green eyes take on the colour of the moss. When the moss moistens and the sun hits the leaves, that are now little stars, I catch a glimpse of my reflection in the lens and wonder what on earth has brought me here, on my knees, in Alys' allotment, staring at the microscopic detail in a moss leaf.

All day, there are moments of detachment, where I am aware of myself from a distance, where I am the one being observed. In the woodland that we walk through on the way home, crouched low over mosses, bemused dog walkers ask us what we are doing. As we explore the cracks in Alys' front wall, bent double over brick with our eyes right up against it, her neighbours make polite enquiries as to our intentions. I am not sure how to answer them – I have no clear hypothesis.

As a horticulturalist, Alys is used to a more scientific approach but, as a writer, shares my investment in hope – without prediction or foreshadowing, just a blush in the bones, gladdening in the proximity of the mosses. Yet, even at this tentative stage, there are visual rewards for those who would join us. If those passing by knew what splendour lay under their feet, millimetres from the ground, if they could see the white hair on a leaf tip, or the neon burst of a fruit stalk, then it might seem extraordinary not to be looking down – to be moving above, oblivious to the setting moss-suns below.

'Is this your favourite moss?' I ask her, looking up from the Fire Moss, ablaze after its wetting, to her hair kindling in the sun. She leans across the vibrant plants in her allotment to pick a brassica leaf.

'For a plate,' she explains, handing it over as we carve up a carrot cake. 'I don't know that I have a favourite – each one I look at takes me in and I feel I could readily jump ship. But it's in a spot that's important to me.' She explains how she walks up and down this path through the winter months, collecting compost from the other end of the allotment. In summer, you wouldn't know the moss was there, but, as it comes into its own from October, for her, it marks the seasons.

'What's also exciting,' she confides, 'is that it grows in the very polluted, non-natural places of pavements. I take solace from that, when I'm feeling trapped in the city.' And I feel, instinctively, that she is right – that I don't have to be in a woodland to feel the pioneering freedom of the mosses. Here, in the city, it is in the cracks of the patio, on the garage roof, under my feet on the way home where the mosses reach me, glossy lights in the tightest of places.

'Do you have to see it under a lens, to get that sense of its impact?' I ask.

'No – but it does become more fascinating when you have an understanding of what it's doing.' And I feel that way too – that the more I learn about mosses, the more extraordinary they become, and, yet, it is the most ordinary of plants too – the most overlooked of lifeforms under my shoe.

'The microscopic detail is where you can feel a large expanse,' Alys says, stretching in the flaring light. 'In a city, it's difficult to find something unexamined. But mosses are truly wild spaces.'

BOLTON FELL

The mosses are latticed with traces of years, hours, seconds, days. At Bolton Fell, a lowland raised bog near Carlisle, time begins to change. While, further off, clusters of snowdrops chime in small blows and catkins in hazel toll over primrose, here, in the mosses, everything slows. Holding onto stillness, the mosses feel like guardians of a quietness that is hard to find and getting harder all the time – although they themselves may be full of the jump of tiny, six-legged springtails; the pull of passing slugs and worms; the busyness of ants; birds landing with a thump; the noise of the water passing through and the sound of spores popping; at their micro-level, these are hidden from high human ears.

The weeks in between my time with Alys and now have been filled with local mosses. Tied to work in the city, there has been no opportunity for wider drifting. I've explored the mosses on the rooftop and in my front doormat, on the pavement by the bus stop and on the concrete slabs across the garden. When these were exhausted, magpies brought me new sources: small deposits gathered on the garden table. Sometimes, when reading in bed, I would hear the thud of a mossy missile meeting its target. When the magpies really meant business, the thud would wake me from sleep. Mosses had entered the rhythm of my days, but I longed for a place they could take up more space. When the chance finally came to move off the clock, I travelled north to enter the time of the bog.

In an instant, the scent of the peat as a base note is softened, smothered with chlorophyll, with sun in light leaf, with the woollen fluffed-up tips, spliced with the silver slice of teeth. There is a deep, earthy crumble and a crumpled tumble of living things like a ball of string, all interwoven. As Sphagnum mosses and other bog plants decompose, they build up layers that eventually form peat. The deeper in, the darker the peat, and the more decomposed the moss. Peatlands are important carbon stores, with the United Nations Environment Programme reporting that they hold twice as much carbon as all the world's forests. If you get close enough, you can access these stores of time. Where the heave of the years has ground down, they may pass now, between the fingers, without resistance.

Yet when peat becomes degraded, if dried out for agricultural practices or extracted for fuel, it releases large quantities of harmful carbon dioxide into the atmosphere. As the UK Peatland Strategy for 2018 until 2040 reports, over 80 per cent of UK peatlands are currently in a degraded state. At Bolton Fell, extraction had left the peat exposed: a bare, dry surface lacking vegetation, susceptible to erosion. In these conditions, water can run quickly off the smooth surface, carrying the peat with it. These benign repositories of healing can be turned on their head from neglect.

As part of an extensive restoration project by Natural England in recent years, the bare peat here has been rewetted and re-vegetated, with Sphagnum mosses playing an important role. In this reciprocal exchange, where human recovery is entwined with the mosses', there is an invitation to think of health differently – wider and more expansively. And it is reassuring to think of those working here, and across other sites of restoration, trialling new ways of living with moss, new strategies for tending to loss. As I stand by the springing quilt the plants have built, it takes all my willpower to move, so much in the mosses is soothed.

When I finally stir, it is, once more, to follow the women in the wetlands. This time, at a conference close to Penrith, Deborah, Bolton Fell's site manager, is speaking. As I enter the room, I find her in front of a projector explaining something to do with peat bunding. Sections of turf-covered peat – *bunds* – can be used to divide areas of bare peat, where there is extensive erosion, into smaller sections. This breaks the area of micro-erosion down into smaller cells, reducing the water flow and wind erosion across the peat. Such a system makes sense to those who grieve, who have known the gusts that batter the body, the relentlessness they can embody. If that hollowness could be broken down, with bunds made of something hopeful placed around, it would become harder for sadness to rule, its dominion could not be so total.

As Deborah's slides give way from peat bunds to Sphagnum mosses, her face changes from concentration to animation. She is speaking now, as one does about friends, things held dear, whatever makes a life worth living. There is a warmth coming from her that matches the fiery colours of the Sphagnum, reminding me of earlier in the year, in Cave Valley, when I had put my hands to the mosses and felt them radiate.

I ask her what first drew her to mosses. She tells me how she became involved with them nearly twenty years ago when she began working for Natural England (then called English Nature) and that they were never the popular sites to work on since they were considered 'difficult' and challenging to visit. She was drawn to the huge amounts of time that they represent – accumulations of peat since the retreat of the last ice age – and couldn't help but feel their primeval history.

The long histories in peat are unique. Where Sphagnum mosses have broken down and compacted, the scope of their histories becomes visible. You can reach your arm down into bog and trace centuries on your risen skin. In place of an arm, a peat core can be used to channel more deeply, establishing a bog's age and collecting specimens that give insights into how the land has changed over time, in some cases showing the impacts of climate change. Corers – semicylindrical chambers comprising a sequence of sections with a blade that twists – are used to cut the peat. The deeper the peat, the more sections are added to the corer. Every core section lifted back up from the peat might cover around 500 years of history. A section from the core's base could show evidence from thousands of years ago.

I ask if she felt an affinity to these places before she started this work – since they have not always been popular places to visit, with tales of people being lost to the bog deeply embedded in Western culture. 'They are a classic Cinderella site – they don't appeal to many and, therefore, are often overlooked. Perhaps I just am drawn to the underdog . . . and I like a challenge!'

I ask about the commercial growing of Sphagnum mosses at Bolton Fell. It was her idea to trial this at the site and the first time it has been used as part of a major peatland restoration project. Deborah is a pioneer here; a torchbearer for bog mosses, as Alys has been for those in the city. I follow their light like a chain, as the glow in me turns to a flame.

'It's a brand-new technique, so we are still watching and learning,' Deborah says. 'We've seen in some areas mosses covering the bare surface within six months.'

'Do you think mosses have a role to play in climate change?' I ask, charged by the thought, yet feeling the disparity between the microscopic mosses and the largeness of the question.

'Simply – yes! A huge role! Peatland habitats and their restoration are a really easy win for keeping carbon in the ground. Coupled with changes in agriculture to adopt paludiculture – wetland farming – they can help curb some of the UKs largest carbon emission sources. This is also true around the world.'

'Do you have a favourite moss – perhaps a Sphagnum at Bolton Fell?' I ask. I am reminded of how her face changed – ignited – when the Sphagnum had entered her slideshow, as she answers.

'I like all the Sphagnum group but perhaps the most beautiful is *Sphagnum pulchrum* . . . not yet established on Bolton Fell moss, but there's time!'

CHRISTOW

How long does it take to become established? My father's side of the family are documented as having lived near Christow, a neighbouring village to Cave Valley in Devon, since the Middle Ages. Two houses are still linked to the family – one farm at the edge of the village, occupied by my great-aunt and her son, and, on the other side, a former farmhouse where my grandmother grew up – now only connected to the family through memory. On the edge of Dartmoor, by hill upon hill of dark woodland, this place drifts into stuffy rooms in Birmingham when I least expect it – sometimes the projector's mirage onscreen summons a distant dance of trees. Other times, the thud of a magpie's dropped moss wakes me from dreams of this green outpost.

At the next opportunity, I take a train from the city, then walk from Cave Valley to Christow and from house to house, following mosses. While most maps use junctions and buildings as navigational aids, I choose these tiny plants. It is a slower way to move but a stronger way to become attuned. Entering the village, the moss at the turning, *Thuidium tamariscinum* (Glowflake), is all over the otherwise dull hedge branches. In this edge from winter towards spring, its yellowy-lime is a heartening thing – a trill of colour in bare bush, a high note in a low slope of wood. Though I am following mosses, I cannot completely ignore the words of this place, as Wet Lane runs parallel to Dry Lane before meeting at a dense acrocarp. Acrocarp mosses grow straight upwards, while pleurocarps grow horizontally. I'm not familiar with this one, dropped in a clump, perhaps by a passing bird, and use a key to help identify it. In this process, called 'keying out', a series of statements are listed in the key that may or may not apply to the moss (such as the nature of the leaves or stems). By following all the statements that are true of the moss, the list of species that it might be can be narrowed down, hopefully leading to the correct one. Coming up as *Racomitrium aquaticum*, Narrow-leaved Fringe-moss, the splayed leaves shower light, firing a cluster of rocket fireworks in my hand.

Moss by moss, I make my way between the houses. More striking *Thuidium tamariscinum* (Glowflake) at the road's curve rhymes with those I had seen earlier, as mosses start to build their own music, playing little repetitions, moments of similarity and difference stuttered through the landscape. At the field edge, spatterings of acrocarps cover the rock walls and I imagine Ann, my great-aunt, brushing past, perhaps, over the years, making contact. I find a pinch of *Tortula muralis* – Wall Screw-moss, following the mosses down, before rounding the corner to my grandmother's childhood house. The front door is open – an invitation I cannot resist, as I look through the open door to a window facing the garden.

Lucy had grown up here in a farming family before moving a few miles north-west to a neighbouring village to marry Wallace, another farmer. As a child, I remember her churning butter and making clotted cream and how one of her sisters would work in the fields. Yet, then, it had been the men that were called farmers and the women, farmer's wives. More recently, in Defra's 2016 Farm Structure Survey, women were shown to make up 55 per cent of the UK's agricultural workforce. With a long history in practice but a short one on record, I wonder how many are in my lineage and how the gap between us might be bridged.

Through the window, immense peaks and troughs of land spread far out into the distance. It is hard to know what to do with such largeness after the small detail of the mosses. Not knowing what to do with my eyes, I let them drift from place to place. They land on the word Archer. They sharpen. Once more, they focus in on detail. Who is to say whether this Archer, on a poster advertising a talk in the village, is one I am related to, if they have any link to my grandmother, Lucy Archer, who used to live where I am standing now. My father, the historian, is no longer here to ask. I remember his words though, that 'the Christow Archers are one of the oldest branches in the Teign valley, but at the same time the most difficult to trace'.

Following mosses, I find the same species recurring at intervals, with surprising newcomers in between. I don't know how each one connects, or doesn't, to the other, as they don't know how I link, or don't, to a family who is here and not here, who is past and present and absent. Still, I trace each one – *Thuidium tamariscinum* (feathery, lime Glowflake in the hedgerows), *Racomitrium aquaticum* (Rocket, the fiery acrocarp from the ditch), *Tortula muralis* (Edge, from the tip of Ann's family's landfall) – to my spot by Lucy's old wall. An abundant acrocarp hugs the rock, its bright sporophytes – tiny capsules holding spores on the top of the stalks – light me like a fuse. The colour fuels.

ROCKET
Racomitrium aquaticum, Narrow-leaved Fringe-moss

Higher
than moon,
lower than grass,
cobweb of leaf, threading
of glass, flammable patchwork
of glowing, fire in water, a sowing
of light in the dark, a seeding of hope
at the start, slow growing of a chance-
led art – to make a locket from a lock,
to break the rocket from the rock.

EDGE

Tortula muralis, Wall Screw-moss

You have your nerves on show,
so that anyone might know
what finds your edges,
or for whom you are smooth,
what turns you reckless,
of whom you approve. Might I
live like that? The silver thread
stretching from my very tip into
others, its tether of impossible courage.

By the open door where one grandmother lived, peering into a past I can only ever glimpse, something slips. The memory of Lucy does not keep me here – I have sensed all I can of the passing of years. It is another grandmother who I think of now – my mother's mother, Isabella, who ran the farmland in Kenya. She was in charge when my grandfather worked away, managing the coffee plantation, the maize and sugar cane. And my mother would pick coffee and collect the milk and the work of these women brushes through me like silk.

EMBU, KENYA

A network is brimming, emerging, a link. My mother's side of the family can be traced back at least 200 years in Embu, to a Rukwara clan leader, and is likely to have been in the area far longer. Not having been there since childhood, I can only see this place through memory. Fragments of it are stored in the nerve cells, still entangled, like a trail of moss. Yet, it is not mosses I follow to get here. Here, it is embers. Bananas baking. Ashes breaking and the glow of the cells re-forming, shaping. In some ways, it is the opposite of looking through a microscope. Memory takes loosening rather than tightening – is something to drift into, not skewer. In other ways, it is its echo. My mother is the lens I slide before my own eyes. Shapes don't make sense until she places them. Hers is the light and the sound and the taste in them.

When I first show her Embu through Google Maps, online in Devon, it is not an instantly heart-warming homecoming.

'Where's this?' I ask, placing the laptop in front of her.

'Exeter?' she answers, not really looking. I ask her to put her glasses on. 'Very messy,' she shakes her head – 'Nairobi?' But then it is there, that spark in the circuit as her face spreads into a smile, 'Embu.' We spend a happy half-hour tracing her old haunts. The map does not extend to the remoter areas, where she used to live, but we see the main parts of the village and its vicinity. We see her old primary school and a hill she once climbed. We see a school named after an 'uncle' who she has been telling me about recently. I have yet to determine his precise relation to the family, but that he was a notable figure in the area and that we were related seem to be facts. It is strange, at first, to be faced with concrete, public evidence of what has previously only been gentle conversation with my mother – here, in bricks and mortar, or whatever the school is made of, which I can't quite determine through a digital map, is my family's mark on the landscape.

I pan further out, to dense forest, and, not far off, to mountain. It seems extraordinary to grow so close to such majestic rock and its awesome presence lies a little further off from me – I feel intimately the pull of hill, wood, wetland but am more remote from this rugged, towering strength. I think of the basalt and manganese in Cave Valley but these are fragments now, small, fallen scree. I keep looking. Here and there, the map shows pockets of mountain that climbers have filmed: little pools and boggy areas. Mosses. Now I am there. Now I have crossed over

Though I cannot get close enough to identify them, their presence is warming and familiar. A local bryophyte report published in 1995 by Min S. Chuah-Petiot records close to 200 species, belonging to 61 families of bryophyte, from Mount Kenya. Conditions are good for mosses in the montane forests where there is high rainfall and humidity. Looking at the blushing peaches and pinks, once more something in me is lit. In the mosses' company, I shift through time, feel the years track along the spine. But, as I draw my moss map, I am conscious that a pioneer should understand what has come before and be prepared to honour, not simply overscore. I zoom back to the locality of the village, as close as possible to my mother's old home. I try to see the coffee plantation and the maize and sugar cane. I try to see the plants that I had once tried so hard to name.

A field of maize brushes up against the buildings. A rough dirt track runs to the side and a major road in front but, it is the maize that is the dominant force, all else is background noise. The field on the map is adjacent to one I have been in, to plants I have brushed past in a childhood rush to the river. The closeness raises a shiver. And memory, too, is like that. Just a nudge away from a connection – years leap-frogged in a single sensation. I had met my grandmother a handful of times. Displaced scenes begin to rise. Her soft commands. Her working hands. Her deep, kind eyes, her laughter lines. Powerful but never far from a good humour that would rush from her like a bursting river. A clutch of rain falls into frame. Joy needs a careful sealant. Time weaves through the maize leaves. Wind heaves through the grazed trees.

3 . CATS' EYES

THE CINDER PATH

Wind heaves through the grazed trees, flooding the fields, warping the windows. *Where are you now?* I ask my father. When the overwhelming force of those lost to us meets the irrepressible force of wind, it feels like it could tear the turf from the ground, whipping the tops clean off the hills. Though I have started to sense sadness relent, to withstand some part of its threat, I cannot afford to be complacent. The wind tries first to remove the windows, then, when that fails, to get in through the gaps along the panes. Joy needs a careful sealant.

I look out to the mosses on the Cinder Path at my childhood home. Beginning where the laurel hedge, planted around the time of my birth, shields the field from the drive, my father wore the path down by walking, while my mother made it the 'Cinder Path' by throwing on ashes from the fire. From the wilderness of the bottom lawn where no one else went, down to the speckled light of the copse, beneath the willow leaves, this path is still one of the first places I go when I think of mosses. In a couple of days, I will return to the Midlands but am relieved to be here on his birthday. When I am away from them, I dream of the places that join us. When I am in them, I am always affected. It is as though something soft is placed around me, a living carpet over the body.

When the worst of the March winds have passed, I check the ground, finding broken boughs, scattered petals, dislocated flower heads, but the mosses, though largely rootless, have stayed in place. Being small has its benefits and this is one of them – in their boundary layer of air, close to the ground, they avoid the higher brunt of violence. As the path becomes more established, so does the moss – fur turns to feather and branches of green snowflakes: *Glowflake*, I whisper, following the tiny lights like markers along a runway.

Moving slowly, in moss time, I ache to read the whole pathway, from source to sea, like a river.

I take out my hand lens, craning deeper into wet grass. The glossy translucence of the leaves is tenuous, inviting touch, yet escaping it. Leaves trickle like water down the spine of the plant, sticking, at intervals along the stem: *Plagiothecium denticulatum*, Dentated Silk-moss. So many of the common names for mosses seem underwhelming but, for once, I think the name is right – that the shining leaves display a magic material. For decades, I have walked over this plant, not noticing that this string of leaves all dressed for dinner in satin and pearls and leafy pressed curls was under me. I can't quite take it in. The scale of the neglect versus the scale of its glamour. It's almost too large to comprehend.

I wonder what it is I am really seeing when I look at this moss. If I can liken it to anything, which I almost can't, it would be that feeling of reading, when words that once seemed so familiar appear to have caught fire and assumed new shapes, startling and extraordinary, yet also not new. Somehow, they are the shapes that I have held in me all along and these words are simply their sparking echoes. It is a feeling of symmetry and strangeness together, an alertness and a familiarity. Though I long to stay in this spot, I force my legs downstream.

Now the moss takes hold of the coal, as chunks are covered with lime-green *Kindbergia praelonga* – which I call Kind Spears. They make strange ornaments. Where the coal is intact and the whole moss plant visible across it, it is like seeing a fossil while it is still alive; the green ribs of the moss leaf against a charred relief. Tips of *Isothecium myosuroides* flash up like jewels from the sea floor – far more glamorous than its common name, Mouse-tail Moss, suggests – this is the Marilyn Monroe of the mosses. I call it Marilyn.

MARILYN

Isothecium myosuroides, Mouse-tail Moss

O furry mouse, o feathered flounce, you catch between soft
paws, you pounce ~ such little wings, such tufted springs, a
bounce ~ a bounce ~ a dance begins. You're a fan that spreads
as heather, sprigs of heath and ostrich feather. Mousy you are
not ~ your glamour has a sleek, seductive power. See the way your
branch is lit and how you move as though leaf tips were hips that
sway ~ your leaves sashay through all the woodland's darker days.

O, you are a moss parade! A firework! A bright cascade
showering light all down your body, who are you? You are
everybody who ever had a heart on show, a vulnerability that
glows in spite of who is looking ~ you're bold. And so I cannot
call you 'mouse' as though I don't see brightness bursting but if
monograms must hold, we'll keep MM with different wording ~
'Mouse-tail Moss' can go but welcome, Marilyn Monroe! The
smoothest moving moss that lived, the lithest and the silkiest. I
take a breath each time I see you, shoulders back, I try to be you.
Who cares if I don't quite make it, just the strength to undertake
it is enough for most let's face it life can be dull and its light
escape us.

What if Marilyn had had her own Marilyn for brightness?
Could we be our own lightness?

Still, I am unsure about this act of naming. I think of my own and how a hyphen lends a way into multiplicity. In Old English kennings, words are joined together – whale-road for sea, sky-candle for sun – so that I start to wonder about kennings for mosses: star-grass; leaf-glass. In Swahili, some words can also be doubled, so that the first impression, rather than being coupled with another, is reinforced. The Swahili word for memory is '*kumbukumbu*'. Again, I feel the microscope lens draw in and pull out – the same thing viewed in different ways – the same word caught in different phases of meaning feels an ideal language for memory.

The path fades into water where the stream seems a sea, high and fast and buoyed by rain. Eyes light on a daisy's sheen, a camellia leans away from its leaves, flowers fall in where mosses recede. When the path ends, you begin again but it is not from the beginning. Like a labyrinth, or meditation walk, the Cinder Path gives a way of moving with thought. I wonder if Alys is on her moss path today, or if Deb is moving over the Sphagnum floor. I think of us joined through our touching of the small.

When I make my way inside the house, *Daddy Long Legs*, a musical with Fred Astaire, is playing. He's singing: 'Something's Gotta Give'. I think of the wind on the pane. I think of the air over mosses. I think of the force of my father and the immovability of a day that persists without him, that would have been his birthday. As objects continue without those they once belonged to; a shell, a shoe, a shore; his birthday still exists without him. There is a residue of him in it that rings like a chorus.

As he neared the end, I was desperate to know where he was at all times. When he seemed to be slipping too far, I would cast out a net and pull with all my might to haul him in again. I felt, then, that he was in the air, in the blackbirds' song; in the fields, the dewy grass tops; in the soil, settled somewhere in the aerated earth. Now, it is not with desperation that I try to find him but curiosity. Where do people go when we lose them? Ridiculous to think they rattle around windows. Impossible to think they float from cloud to cloud, looking down. So many of the places we make for our dead read like parts of a children's story, fables that persist into adulthood. The space he takes up now is in the earth, yes. But it is in the air, too. The mosses, in their close proximity to earth, breathe by him. Theirs is the air he feels coming and going, in his own, protected boundary layer.

Mum joins me in watching the musical. Its whirl is infectious and we start to hum. It is only a little noise, a small throb of air from the space at the back of the throat, yet it feels wider than wind, more expansive. And while it is there, there is no room for anything else. Tiny tremors of light along the throat, along the earth. Mosses are the music that carries me to him. The low pulse between two worlds.

THE BOUNDARY LAYER

A slow rock as the neck unfurls and a bounce rises from the toes. Where I stand by the grave, less than a mile from the Cinder Path, *Rhytidiadelphus squarrosus*, Springy Turf-moss, has begun to grow. I pull myself forward. Sometimes it is the smallest of movements that has the largest impact. In this forward fold, some days I can reach my toes, other times the shins, today, it is just a little past the knees. There is so much hooked up in the torso, so much savaging the spine. I bend the knees and heave my chest towards them, my hands wrap my feet and there is relief. I stay in this position for a few minutes, not wanting to leave the feeling of weightlessness. Although I am still with the hurt, it is the difference between being pulled and pummelled in the periphery of the storm and being truly, deeply inside, in its middle, where there is a kind of cushioning. There is a relief in saying, this is the loss that I could sense but not fully feel. This is what I have been carrying, in this tiny increment of spine over knee, it is all here, in the nod of my head, in the tiny bend of me.

I let my hands touch the mosses and lower my knees. Sending my weight forward, I twist and turn my head to ground. Ear-level with the mosses, I strain to hear. If there is a speech that I can access, it is in movement. In the motion of air trickling through leaves, in the leaping bellies of springtails, the slow evaporation of water. I stay in the twist. In this gentle slip of a body softening, the mosses spread like clouds under the head, lapping. Drumming. There is no need to do anything but sink into the beat of the leaves. As the air strums, I feel myself lift. There is a momentum that comes from the pit of the stomach and the flip of the green and the swell of the seas, equally. The mosses foam and teem, lilting as I am lifting, and the air circles around and threads between. There is a weaving of wind and a lean into it, like an intimate folding, like holding.

SEA WRINKLE

Rhytidiadelphus squarrosus, Springy Turf-moss

And the hills move
    and the earth churns
and the flame chars
    and the chalk burns
and the weeds cast
    their waves towards us
and we all of us
    pull up from water
leaves lain in the darkness
    sea wrinkle and harness
of feather in night
    stone-quiet.

TOR ROYAL, DARTMOOR

The light unfolding draws me out, on my last day in Devon for some time. Nearby, Fox Tor Mire has found fame as the treacherous Grimpen Mire in Conan Doyle's *The Hound of the Baskervilles*, but there is no such sense of foreboding here. I pass Tor Royal, the only raised bog – where the peat forms a dome – in the county. As I walk, an orange, waning moon over moor gathers me gently and thaws the tight muscles of mourning. Bright stars, cold air, a deep freshening – the emptiness makes a lasting impression. You meet yourself on the moors, where the limits are all yours – the lack of height, vertical objects, cover or shade, can be relentless or alluring, depending on what is made of them.

As the sun peaks, I reach an ancient burial site, a Bronze Age kistvaen that would have likely once held a cremation. With some original lining slabs and the capstone still there, along with stones from the retaining stone circle, its glare reflects the shine of the day as the score of the night melts away and into this site of the Crock of Gold, I feel the bog mosses rise up and take hold. The Fringed Bog-moss with its alpine breath and Lustrous Bog-moss in its ballet dress throb inside like a risen sun, bob and dive in a moorland song. In summer, high-rising skylarks and low-lying pools will be joined by dragonflies lit up like jewels. Just now, the movement is duller, the mosses providing the most colour.

While the stones hug the landscape like the peat itself – remnants of the dead that don't go on somewhere else – the mosses urge me to move on. Their trail is a softer one. I think of my father's resting place, some miles away, where I followed the moss and felt the sway of a different rhythm. Now I move to the beat of the moss, and walk on, a few miles north. I reach a woodland that pulls me off-path.

ALPINE BREATH
Sphagnum fimbriatum, Fringed Bog-moss

Apple mint, little glint, twisting all among the chintz – flecked with
cream and churns of greening, scoops of wax and humus teeming
    alpine breath and ice-cream leaf – the pistachio of peat – tendrils of an old
man's whiskers wrapped around the reeds in whispers of brisk peppermint
    high skips of colour in the mire – fresh drift of summer stored inside –
ready to release, ever alert to disturbance by wing, a trembling thing or burst
    of nearing.

WISTMAN'S WOOD

Through the bark, something is rising. Boundaries are breaking. If mosses line the border between the living and the dead, then moss people – the moss-covered wood sprites from German and Scandinavian folklore – mark the mind and forests' edge. Where imagination meets landscape, where spirit meets leaves, here there is a suspension of belief.

These characters embody the human fascination with mosses, showing how, for centuries, the proximity of these plants to earth and tree has so intrigued that it has even triggered a sense of their animation. Often depicted as small humans covered in moss with unruly hair resembling lichen, the moss people of German folklore had the ability to both plague or heal the land. In Golther's *Germanische Mythologie*, moss-women, or 'wood ladies' are said to have come out of the forest during epidemics to show people the plants that could cure them.

As I move through Wistman's Wood, I remember it is known for its deep affiliation with mosses. The high oaks, on the banks of the west Dart, are steeped in them. Its name, perhaps derived from the local dialect 'wisht', meaning 'eerie', or even, some suggest, 'haunted' or 'pixie-led', seems to invite the uncanny. If moss people were to be found anywhere, one feels, it would be here. Sometimes featured as the object of the mythical Wild Hunt (a ritual known to many cultures, involving the rising up of the dead to travel together over the land), to escape, they would enter the trees. In a particular Devonshire iteration of this tale, the mythical hellhounds belonging to the Devil are said to reside in Wistman's Wood and to run out from it as part of the hunt.

Reports of those spending time here are not favourable. Children are lost. Adults are chased by hellhounds, while those daring to lie in the mosses risk the wrath of disturbed adders. Yet, if you have lost someone, if you know someone resting beneath the earth, you may find yourself drawn to places where the boundary between life and death appears slim – to those small points where the ground caves in. And such places are not always to be feared. In Japan, moss gardens are prized. Following the aesthetic of *wabi-sabi*, which values imperfection, moss is seen as a kindred spirit with its seemingly random, asymmetrical patterns of growth. Deeply symbolic within Buddhism, there are moss gardens containing statues dedicated to the spirits of the dead. In these traditions, the connection to the departed is not one to be feared – it is a tranquil, soothing, opening.

Lying in the mosses, I watch them blanket the bark above, where the air washes the leaves and sunlight slips between the eaves. The tors on the moor have broken down, eroded into smaller versions of themselves, falling, until coming to rest here, in the broken rock known as clitter. Beneath my back, the ragged rock is softened by the mosses and they, in turn, are strengthened by the rock. The heart in the ribs slows and the sun seeps through the back in golden waves. There is wind and there is cold, but, at the moss's edge, I am folded over with warmer air and the feeling that there are gentle forces at work, just as much as the furious. In my small boundary layer, metres below the storm, I catch only the sunlight, I know only warmth.

I know that there are ways of slipping between the elements and that not all are reckless. Not all have adders and hellhounds and windows that rattle. Some are smooth and silken and all that matters is that you give yourself over to them fully – that you trust in where you are going, although you are only following. It is not for you, in these moments, to direct the flow of the body – you need only not stand in its way. The mosses pulse and sway, tiny telephones, connecting you to whatever may be restless.

From the Cinder Path to Wistman's Wood runs a straight, southwesterly line. From my newly discovered jewels of *Isothecium myosuroides* (Marilyn) and *Plagiothecium denticulatum* – Dentated Silk-moss (Gentle Fire) along the path, to the smatterings of

Leucobryum juniperoideum, Smaller White-moss and *Antitrichia curtipendula*, Pendulous Wing-moss that greet me here, the mosses mark my route like cats' eyes. In the remotest catchments: moss. In the crowded pathways: moss. In the line between earth, air and my father, mosses feather the way. My shoulders sink and neck nestles in Pendulous Wing-moss. I feel the body swing along this stretch of Devon earth. No matter how far it is taken, it returns.

INBETWEENER
Antitrichia curtipendula, Pendulous Wing-moss

I weave.
I plait and spin, held in the wings, measuring
the distance
between moments, anchored in the deep lowness
before
leaping. I am a vein, creeping its way back to the heart
after
its big night out in the dark, clawing against the door for
a chance
to get back in. I am tinged with impulse and yearning,
I am before
and after the burning, nothing can be done to stir me.
I thieve.

GENTLE FIRE

Plagiothecium denticulatum, Dentated Silk-moss

Golden gloss, sea shimmer, small glimmer. Stem of suns, sugar-spun – as if each sun were hung from a washing line, billowing pillows of light – in beams, tracking the seas of the underneath.

At the same time, you are a working moss. Nobody does it for you. Gold does not appear dropped at your door in the night with a note, it is hard-won and hard-fought, it is you and you alone who forged it from a life that might not have otherwise made it. You are your own favourite. If you outclass the field that is not your concern, you are healed of all comparison. Peerless. You come in dreams like a fearless desire, with gentle fire, you steer towards success. For you, that means more than your dress, albeit silk and covered in flecks of precious metal, for you it is not having to settle for anyone else's idea of a life.

Some call you leafstrong. As if it were bad to have a strong leaf. You do not listen to dull speech. You are tuned to a higher music and do not abuse it with baser chatter. What does it matter what anyone thinks, when you live in gold and silver and clink your leaves together like a bat? There is nothing flat about your endless campaign against the toss of the waves, again and again, to rise in soft flames is a spectacle I cannot tire of. To see you shot through with light, and never switched off, is a rallying call to the parts of myself that are soft to push to the top and not stop.

We all have it in us – the capacity not to be dimmed – so each time I see you I begin again. My light fuel. My bright renewal. I look up to you.

CHIME
Leucobryum juniperoideum, Smaller White-moss

Restless shine, half-chime
over breathing bark, sub-song
of the throttled dark, roots rubbing
rainbows under growth, trembling
sheens among the oaks, trampled
whispers in the earth half-spoken
and rehearsed in ground to surface
again twice as loud: *if there's anything
that you need, then please* – step back
and the sound recedes, press on
as the voices plead.

Lying in my moss bed, I see no sprites – hear no thud of hellhounds' hooves – the only sound in the mosses soothes. In the boundary layer, I am cushioned. At this small scale, the elements loosen. When I speak to my father, it is not with the voice but stretches of skin that let the water in. I soak in his presence. Light channels its bloodless speech; in the mossy fretwork, words run fast and fleet. Our fingers meet. For a second, there are something like fingers. For a moment, something like touch. Then, the burst. Leaves disperse. The sudden pelt of petals.

4. SMALL SKIES

The sudden pelt of petals when sadness falls and settles is beguiling. It draws you in. This is the stealth by which it moves: first it comforts, then removes all your defences. It may feel good, at first, to sink into a wound. But it will take up your empty spaces and expand, lengthening but narrowing, until you are one long causeway, exposed and all-too susceptible to the elements. Stretched, in the fathomless wetness, the loss runs fast and deep. When this happens, it helps to find a model – something that looks like you to follow.

The Sweet Track in the Somerset Levels is one of the earliest known wooden causeways. Built by Neolithic farmers, it was part of a network of tracks used to navigate over marsh. I think of it often as the weeks pass. Bound to the city and long working hours, I feel the body hollowing out. Parts that had repaired start to splinter and tear. On the Sweet Track, poles of alder and hazel were driven into the ground with ash, oak and lime planks placed in between, held fast by pegs. Sometimes, friendship can keep you from sinking. But when you show up stretched out by sadness, some may not recognize you. They may not know how to respond, or what to do with you. Pegs come loose.

Yet, friends who are used to being astonished will not mind your shapeshifting. And so it is good to be regularly amazed. Then you won't mind when your friends show up like the tangled and strewn offerings of a cat. You will still see them. Then you won't mind when your friends show up flat, like the planks of a track. You will still feel them. Then you won't mind when your friends don't show up at all. You will understand that somewhere along the length of them, a peg has come loose and you will know what to do.

AVALON MARSHES

An egret beats through, white oars in the blue, sky-sculling. I have spent so long looking down, I have forgotten about sky; so caught up in routine, I have not felt its light. When I think of Camilla's flexibility in meeting me here, at short notice, without any solid plan, I glimpse her egret life, large and soaring. A poet friend, words first brought us together, though now there is much more that binds us. I want to show her the mosses, to bring her into their lightness.

Looking deep into the glittering water, I am revelling in having a day away, when she calls to say she's been walking the wrong way. I laugh and apologize for my directions. I think of the difficulty of poets meeting anywhere – the shift required from the flesh of words to the flat mapping of space. But when we meet it is all laughter and spring sunlight. I follow her swift movement as she strikes out along the path. She hears a reed warbler; I hear a sedge. Back and forth, we exchange our senses.

She is soon talking, derisively, about the reduction of mosses to their sex lives in much of the literature she has read. 'The way they go on about SPLASH CUPS!' she roars, shaking her head so her long hair flies loose, and I'm laughing too, as we stride off onto the Sweet Track. Following the path that was once an ancient pilgrim route, we exchange recipes for life – how much time is spent writing, how much on other work, and how to redress the balance. Now and then we dip off-track. In the dark glen, goat willows have knotted over to cover a flash of water and dense cushions of mosses. Camilla splashes down, bending low to see what grows. There are many I don't know here. My fingers play their extraction scales – how much could be taken, how much could be lost – as I take pictures rather than samples to help to key them out. *Campylopus introflexus*, Heath Star-moss, papers the bark. With its distinctive white trailing hair, it is hypnotic. The mosses grow so healthily in this spot, singing their green from stream to sky. In the fringes, hidden from most human eyes, they seem to thrive.

Lifting our eyes from the mosses, through the willows, over the reeds to the water, we sense the gold pouring in. Our legs follow and we find ourselves back on the path. But I can't stop there. In among the tall, straw-like reeds I flit, 'Like King Alfred, hiding in the reed beds,' Camilla says, laughing. My thoughts turn to Arthur. Avalon, the legendary island, first appearing in Monmouth's *History of the Kings of Britain*, is where Arthur's sword was forged and where he was taken when mortally wounded. Some believe that before the Somerset plains were drained, Avalon was the site of Glastonbury Tor.

I flutter in the gold, a little distance from my friend. My mourning wound does not seem so deep here, where *Cryphaea heteromalla*, Lateral Cryphaea, fans out from the branches there is lightness and laughter and a sense of what might come after. As we re-join each other, coming to rest in the slow stretch of sun over water, our hands move to pens in unison, as we start to write. It is so different to the time I have begun to spend with scientists in different wetlands, who want to understand from the outset what we are about. Here there is an easy drift between talk and silence, stillness and movement. By the edge of the water, we take in all that is passed to us and leave behind what we still cannot reach.

MERLIN

Campylopus introflexus, Heath Star-moss

Sea-hill, soil-hair,
hoar-leaf, swell-swear
an oath in a fertile pocket
an inflorescent promise
gathered in violets and torn
from fretted rhizoids born
in trailing burst of low stars
where the milk tooth flowers

call it a spell or a longing
call it a debt or a song
in a language hidden
from sight, call it birth-right
in bubbling undercurrent
its trembling powers.

Wordlessly, we re-join the track. Occasionally, I glimpse an unfamiliar moss and follow, until the path peters out into a bright meadow. There are wild flowers everywhere catching the sunlight. Early purple orchids, meadow buttercups, cuckoo flowers. We fall to our knees in order to see them. Our heads droop. Our bodies simulate an act of prayer, centuries old, preserved in the marshes. Neolithic and Bronze Age artefacts have been found in the peat here, beside the tracks. Bronze axes, polished jadeite, perhaps offered, as Richard Brunning reports in *Wet & Wonderful: The Heritage of the Avalon Marshes*, to the gods of the wetlands.

What comes to mind now, is a prayer for the Cave Valley mosses. For, that day, earlier in the year, when I had twice walked away from their dense bodies, determined not to disturb them, I had returned. A nip here, a tug there. I had lifted a sprinkling of mosses from the rocks, carried them all the way back to Birmingham in my rucksack. There, I had tipped them into a plant pot and placed them on my desk. I had watered them, spoken to them and worried about them. Eventually slipping them into the lining of my 'moss shoes', they became a small, wild comfort in my citied days. 'Forgive me,' I whisper to the marshes. 'I'll look after them,' I say to the grass. 'I'll return them,' I promise, with bowed heart.

SLOUGH

Cryphaea heteromalla, Lateral Cryphaea

Create in me a new clean: a heart of fern,
a clinging green, that I might build a new uprightness
that I might carry true bloodlightness through all the curves
of my days, through the willow, the elder, the graze of ash on the corner
where the full tree grows no more and even as I am held up, let the old clean drop.

WEST SEDGEMOOR

The clouds part as I look up, scanning meadow after meadow slop-
ing into the horizon and the Quantock Hills, before messaging M.

'I'm lost.'

'Excellent.'

Living in nearby counties – the West Midlands and Derbyshire –
we intersect at wetlands. Where he is brought by birds, I come for
mosses. West Sedgemoor boasts the greatest lowland population
of breeding wading birds in the south of England and the reserve
is part of England's largest remaining wet-meadow system. M is
keen to hear about the birdlife but I have been mostly keeping my
head at ground-level – so much so, that any broader navigation
has been displaced.

He asks if I need him to pull up a map. As I look at the long,
glinting drains through the meadows, there is, for a second, a
shadow – a sense that I could be taken along their channels and
lose all original shape. But the moment breaks. I remember how I
have walked such narrow causeways with Camilla, have learned
how not to disappear. The peat underneath is over six metres deep.
There is a tension between pulling down and flattening out, a kind
of vertigo, as I move between light water and the dark breath of
the banks. It is up to me to choose which side to follow. To flit in
the shallows, or let the land swallow the parts that don't want to
stay up. In these moments, companionship can save the body from
being reckless, reminding it of the porous possibilities of skin.

I press my ear to the phone and lean into M's voice. It washes
over like a warm current, and, for a moment, takes me with it. As
I move past black sedge and *Brachythecium rutabulum* – Rough-
stalked Feather-moss, I smile. It is a moss I have on my doorstep
in Birmingham, yet have travelled hundreds of miles just to find
again. I think of M back in the Midlands. Radio waves travelling
at the speed of light, even as my feet fix firm in the bright pull of

the mosses. There is a feeling of crossings, extensions and catches, embraces and patches of happiness growing unbidden. How many connections are hidden from the human eye and ear, how many touches in the meadows reach out, then disappear without notice?

Bent down low, I follow the ground around to find it glossed with *Calliergonella cuspidata*, Pointed Spear-moss. And amid the water's shining flourishes, M's question resurfaces. Used to navigating on my own, I don't need another to steer me home, and yet, it is good to feel near to someone here, in the flattened expanse of the mere. I look up to the sight of a crane in the reeds and up further still to two hobbies that reel and whirl in the wind, flaunting stamina, safe back from Africa. Then, back to the ground where leaves cast their light up, small skies spreading their sun through the rough.

'I'm OK,' I say, 'being lost.'

HOME FIRES
Brachythecium rutabulum, Rough-stalked Feather-moss

If lost in a forest, if held in the dark, if caught underwater, if
coming apart, there are ways to surface, there are heaps of breath,
there are leaves that are burnished and strung with strength,
stretching and stirring in the mulchy depths, full of a comfort that
you don't know yet – the patter of velvet paws, the opening of
a thousand doors onto the place you have walked to night after
night, you knew it was there waiting for you – your life.

SWORDFISH
Calliergonella cuspidata, Pointed Spear-moss

Feathered swords, basking in the surface of the soil
breaching only moments in the broil of burning green,

summer in a hundred leaves, autumn pulling down
its sleeves as honey breathes into the branches

tired of carrying a fight they never started – see now
how their blades are only wings, hear now how their
touching softly swings.

GRIMLEY GRAVEL PITS

On my birthday, I am pulled from routine by Louise. A lecturer in philosophy at my workplace, it has been her wont to pick me up and move me along when I've needed it. One of our early adventures had taken us to Cadair Idris, a place where legend, and the poet Robert Graves in *The White Goddess*, says that 'whoever spends the night is found in the morning either dead, mad, or a poet'.[3] It had seemed the ideal spot for a philosopher and a poet to meet. Often, on these excursions, we would walk or climb for a while before I would swim. Sometimes, we'd read poems.

In Felicia Hemans' 'The Rock of Cader Idris', she describes how the 'tongue hath no language to speak what I saw, Things glorious, unearthly, pass'd flooding before me, / And my heart almost fainted with rapture and awe' (ll. 10–12).[4] As we had read it then, surrounded by rock and heather and wild angelica and the slope of the scree and the thrumming of bees, there had been a sense of reciprocity – returning Hemans' words to a place she had felt them falter. The swim at Cadair Idris ranks among my all-time favourites. The cool mountain water, slipping off into the valley at the end of the pool, the feeling of being a tiny light in a dark depth.

Now mosses, tiny lights in dark soil, in peat, on bark, have joined in our journeys. I have begun to train my eyes towards the ground and to keep them there for as long as it takes to learn something of their ways. Today, as we follow one of the Severn Valley bird migration routes, we share the spring air with oystercatchers, little ringed plovers, lapwings and dunlin. Every now and then, Louise stops to points out a common tern. She leans into their flight, her light frame swaying. Their gently lapping wings are so in keeping with the water that they move above.

And we share the ground with Marilyn, Kind Spears, Home Fires and several acrocarps. I trace the little stars of *Polytrichum formosum* – Bank Haircap, seeing Louise's eyes light from their shine before lifting mine to *Polytrichum commune*, Common Haircap, a mass of shooting stars. By watching the ground, I can see the sky; by looking down, I start to rise. The mosses cause a shift in me, small skies lifting me.

SHOOTING STAR
Polytrichum commune, Common Haircap

Blaze, blaze, low meteor
burning through the forest floor,
slip through rock and summer's rust
your trail of fading diamond dust.
Blaze, blaze, low meteor
burning through the forest floor.

When the sun above is gone,
when light can't be relied upon,
then you shoot your molten rock
under nettle, up through dock.
Blaze, blaze, low meteor,
burning through the forest floor.

On our walk back, I find a huge tangle of mosses. In amongst the Marilyn and Kind Spears, gleams my favourite – Glowflake. Dropped, perhaps by a bird that had been squirrelling it for a nest. I pick it up and carry it with me a while as we walk, my little furry birthday present. But it doesn't feel right to take it away and I leave it a few metres on from where I found it, or from where it had found me. Yet, there is something in these chance intersections. The moss dropped on my path, my fingers handling it, before letting it pass. It is not, perhaps, the rapture and awe that Hemans felt at Cadair Idris but the little shimmer of a connection that simmers under the surface, that can happen anywhere – in a garden, on the pavement, on a path, in a gravel pit. When the 'tongue hath no language to speak what I saw' there are other ways to communicate and the body knows them all. The dusting of moss on my palm is small but speaks to me with a thin, wild call.

CAVE VALLEY

In the spin of all that's glowing, I trace the different mosses. Through the weeks since I was last here, I have started to feel more connected. There are people I have chosen and who have chosen me, and, between us, we have tacitly agreed not to let the other go under. As the small skies of the mosses remind me to look up, so a friend's company can release what has been stuck. I am lifted when beside them, with broader horizons.

Now, as I move between clusters, I wonder what each bond is. Is it anything like friendship? Our own gathered communities allow us to share resources more readily, as mosses, who are rootless, are better able to retain moisture in groups. Unable to soak up water through roots, they must be careful to retain it when rainfall reaches their leaves. By growing together, they increase the surface area available to catch and hold onto rain. But could there, as well as such efficiency, be anything else at play?

As one of the most common UK mosses, Kind Spears (*Kindbergia praelonga*), is frequently found growing on logs, on the ground, along the trunks and branches of trees. While Marilyn (*Isothecium myosuroides*) is less ubiquitous, they can most often be encountered on tree trunks and boulders. In the Potawatomi indigenous belief system Robin Kimmerer outlines in *Gathering Moss*, there is a belief that plants show themselves to humans where they are needed. Here, in Cave Valley, just as on the Cinder Path and at the Worcestershire gravel pits, I find them growing together. Why is Kind Spears so often coupled with Marilyn?

While there is still much to learn about the chemistry of mosses, Kind Spears is believed to possess anti-fungal, anti-microbial, cardiotonic and tumour-affecting chemicals. I wonder if Marilyn possesses any such qualities, or whether, in fact, it is the healthful qualities of either species that calls me to them. Being with plants can lower human levels of the stress hormone cortisol and raise the feel-good neurotransmitters of serotonin and dopamine. Yet, how mercenary an exchange it would be, were I simply drawn to them on account of a physical need. I wonder, too, what I might bring the mosses, whether there could ever be a reason for their hoping to see me.

I think of the reciprocity that writing might enable, in building awareness of what the mosses give, and, once more, of my Kenyan relations' name for me, the 'Doctor', on account of my childhood plant potions. I have always been drawn to plants' properties and thought about how they are received. When I ask Mum what she remembers about plants being used for healing, she speaks about doctors of plants and '*wadaktari wachawi*' – the witchdoctors.

'We would have to run very fast past the sugar cane that was poisoned by the witch,' she reveals, nonchalantly. But there were positive plant doctors, or healers, too, who used plants more beneficially. 'You had to know the good ones from the bad ones,' she explains. With many of Kenya's traditional herbalists now advanced in years, there is a risk that this indigenous medicinal knowledge could die with them.

Some documentation of traditional herbalists in the areas around Mum's old home, provided by Kareru, Kenji, Gachanja, Keriko and Mungai in 'Traditional Medicines among the Embu and Mbeere Peoples of Kenya', shows one of the most common plants used for healing to be *Terminali brownii* or, in Swahili, *'mbarao'* or *'mwalambe'*. This leafy, deciduous multi-purpose plant can be used to treat a wide variety of ailments. Although Mum doesn't recall it, she does remember *'quinini'* – quinine – growing locally, and how my grandmother, Isabella, would pick it to add to chicken broth to ward off malaria, as well as a tree with sap that was used for soap – when walking past it, you could see the suds rising. 'Bad' plant doctors were not consulted in the ethnobotanical research I have quoted, whose authors note that 'Non-Christian herbalists were said to combine herbal medicines with witchcraft and were therefore avoided'.[5] There are gaps in the record where we don't know what grows. There are gaps in the explored where nobody goes.

Tetraphis pellucida and *Dicranum flagellare* are two mosses Robin Kimmerer describes as sharing an ability to grow together in 'disturbance gaps'[6] – spaces in the landscape that emerge after a catastrophic disturbance, such as storm or fire. Some mosses, who might struggle in heavily populated spaces where they need to compete, can do well in newly opened disturbance gap ground. I think of the body in mourning as a disturbance gap – a place that has suffered a disaster but that carries on. In such a space, mosses might grow and fledgling feelings flow – sprinklings of joy that, elsewhere, might be shouted down, can here find quieter ground.

As the mosses grow in me – without their physical bodies but with all the pleasure their proximity brings – the body tills the ground for new life to spring. Kind Spears and Marilyn and I grow together. I wonder if the exchanges between us will ever go both ways. Perhaps, if the mosses are elevated with praise – I note Kind Spears with their gentle strength, and Marilyn with their suppleness – as they, in turn, erase the mourning body's heaviness, perhaps there might be a way to be of service – to receive their gift and to return it.

Through the leaves, air shifts and ferns glint. Towards the cave, pennywort, or navelwort, grows with Kind Spears in the rough rock crevices. The common name, 'navelwort' and scientific name, *Umbilicus*, indicate the shape of its round leaves with a dip in the centre. When it flowers, the spike grows from the centre of the leaf, leaving behind a navel-shaped depression. Thought to be able to help the immune system, with antiseptic qualities that can be used for treating wounds, it could be considered a friend to humans but I wonder how it might relate to mosses.

A member of the Stonecrop family, or *Crassulaceae*, it stores water in its fleshy leaves, hoarding the moisture so as not to dry out in times without rain. Moss knows what it's like to store water in your body. Moss leaves, that may only be a single cell thick, absorb the rain and, for a time, keep it safe. Perhaps it is this shared need that binds them. Although pennywort has roots, they are shallow. Both plants know the struggle to hold onto what seems to come easily to more deeply rooted neighbours.

Here, the rock is wet to touch, as water seeps through, plumping the pennywort and soaking the mosses. Kind Spears absorbs so much moisture that its features change – from sharp-leaved spears to a mop of seaweed. Deeper inside the cave, the pastel lichen shimmer the walls and water falls loose like a fan of hair. But the pennywort and mosses grow further out, more bathed in brightness, more a part of a landscape shared with humans. I think about how friendships establish.

Already lifted in their presence, I don't have to look into their eyes or listen for their laugh or tone of voice to test their energies or compatibility. There are no such human registers here. The heart's energy moves beyond the human. It is not restricted to our particular pulse of muscle and valve but pours through the plasticity of leaf and cell. And the pennywort, with its bank of navels, speaks of how that impulse, that lightning assessment of energy that is liking, comes, so often, from the centre of the body – that it can be a gut decision who we join with.

When we think about the plants that grow together, we speak of their needing the same kinds of habitat, growing where they can get hold of the resources they require, perhaps sharing resources through specific acts of mutualism. Undoubtedly, this is part of it. But might this liking also count as a form of mutualism – when we choose to be around beings who make us feel good, who, for whatever reason, leave a positive impression?

KIND SPEARS
Kindbergia praelonga, Common Feather-moss

Small sky, raised high in a light-box of leaves,
heaving neon flickers I long to retrieve – something
of spears in the shape of the bite, something that's
kind in the shape of the light – well-disposed to air
and earth equally, open to others' hurt deliberately
staying after everyone has left, a tenderness.

Leaping in quick succession, in and out of their leaves, springtails are one of mosses' closest companions. Small, wingless arthropods, up to ten millimetres long, their jumping organ, the furcular, is held in place by hooks beneath the abdomen. When released, the furcula springs free, causing it to leap into the air – an action reflected in its common name. They can be found in soil, sand, leaf litter, under bark and stones, in tree canopies and caves. Some inhabit ant and termite nests and, in the latter, are thought to control fungal growth. Here, as they vault through Marilyn, I wonder what they're taking in. Like mosses, springtails can be used as bio-indicators of environmental change, being sensitive to any changes in the toxic elements present in soil, water and air; though I hesitate to reduce their bodies to a gauge.

There is something infectious about them. Soon the jump in the leaf is a jump in the feet and a leap like a scent into air. There is nothing settled anywhere. Perhaps it is this quality that binds them. The moss, that has no roots, and the arthropods with tails like sharp inhales. When the springtail comes in and says *Sing!* Where the springtail comes, singing *Fling!* Where the springtail flings, singing *Spring! Here, in the body, perpetually!* How can you, then, stay woven?

The springtail's standard method of moving is crawling. Perhaps a springtail only jumps when disturbed, or when alert to danger. Not jumping for joy but with fright. No giddy abandonment but the tightening of awareness, the necessary shrinking of space we all face when threatened. I think of all the leaping lessons I have learned. How to make myself small, how to dodge burns. How to play dead, then suddenly swerve. Sometimes, a friend's brightness can help you forget, other times their light is what lets you connect to what you have hidden. They lend you the strength to keep digging.

I envy the springtail's ability to live inside moss. I wonder if it is like walking through a rainforest but one that is soft and plush as well as moist and lush. Perhaps it is like the foothills of

Mount Kenya where Mum remembers the humid drift of the days.
I remember only fragments of that place. Running down the path
of the coffee plantation. Balancing on a plank over a muddy, swell-
ing river; everything tinged sepia. But Mum remembers something
moving in the bush. Not a leopard, she says, though, nevertheless,
a threat. It is a memory that leaps, like a springtail, for one moment
before retreating, back down to its hiding place. It leaves a trail of
dappled light on a path, it leaves something moving in the grass.

5 . STARFISH

UPTON WARREN

Something moving in the grass shifts the ground where we pass. Reeds shuffle in tiny gasps. I trail my fingers atop the grass heads, while Louise's hair flies up, golden in the billowing. At the Upton Warren Nature Reserve in Worcestershire, some 35 miles south of Birmingham, the North Moors Pools have fresh water and the South Flashes Pools are saline. It is rare to find these mixed conditions in such close proximity and this thwarting of established binaries attracts me immediately. We glimpse the water through peach grass. Soft and plush as well as moist and lush. I write in the dappled light, as Louise looks through her binoculars.

'Two tufted ducks,' she reveals. I follow her eye, without the aid of a lens, to the black and white bobbing and ease into the slow drift of things spilling in and things drawing off. A static moment in the moving shore where there is no need to do anything anymore. No desire to move. No thirst for things removed. Just this blue and this black and my friend and two ducks.

The tufted duck is the UK's most common diving duck. I watch them dip under, then slowly resurface, rhythmically, hypnotically. It seems a better arrangement of a life – this daily, hourly, frequent breaking of the surface, a constant flouting of boundaries – than our human attachment to air. We pull ourselves reluctantly from this early viewing point to move further along the path. I trace the mosses beneath our feet.

Among the first plants to evolve out of the water, mosses are still so much a part of it. As non-vascular plants, they lack the vascular tissue to transport water and nutrients around their bodies, and their male reproductive cells also need water to swim in, in order to survive. But when they do obtain it, through rainfall, they are excellent hoarders. Sphagnum mosses can absorb up to twenty times their body weight. I think of the water I hold inside, its gentle wash, its lapping tides. Wetness calls to wetness through the skin. Reviving. Renewing. Brewing.

The closer we get to the water, the more dramatic it becomes. The honk of swans, the frenetic beating of wings. Canada geese with their furious outpourings. Black-headed gulls, Mediterranean gulls, cormorants in a quieter backdrop. Acrocarp turns to pleurocarp the further down we go and a log covered in Marilyn with a tiny spattering of Kind Spears growing in the middle attracts me – these two mosses together again, augmenting my knowledge of what makes us friends. As we move towards the bird hide, I see more Marilyn, this time displaying vivid stalks and red capsules from which spores will release as part of its reproduction process. I think of all this love in the margins, the tiny relationships forming.

The hide is the perfect place to write. Warm wood encloses us – myself, Louise and a man who announces that he's seen a grasshopper warbler.

'Right, I'll be off,' he says, without moving. Time stalls as we sit in the embryonic warmth of the hide with nothing but the movement of birds and water outside and the stillness of our watching bodies inside. Gulls shudder and swoop in and out of the lake as the chime of church bells falls in. There is movement everywhere. The gulls are so loud now, as they sort out breeding territory. There is attraction everywhere. The glowing moss capsules underfoot, the reeling gulls overhead. The wind blows the sound of the bells in and each note hangs pristine in the air that is shared with so much. There is touching everywhere. Air against tongue, vocal chords, wings. We follow a great black-backed gull over the water and Louise says that some but not all gulls migrate to escape our winters and that it seems to be down to individual preference.

Why do some of us choose to live with sadness? Do we forget that we can move, that what tethers us to a place might be challenged and diverted from, if it's for our own good? It is not always possible. There is not always choice. But sometimes, there can be adjustment. Sometimes, a small voice rises and tries, however much it may be talked over, to guide. As we move around the reserve, from fresh water to saline, two sand martins show us the way, quick in the air, flashing. I follow the swoop of the gulls' bodies and the tang of their cries as we arrive at a new hide and find it full.

'I used to dread people asking if there's much about,' Louise confides, 'I wouldn't have a clue.' She started learning more about birds during a period of illness. Unable to get outside, the pages of her bird guide filled the room with teeming skies. Now, whatever I ask her about, she has the answer ready. Every now and then she passes me her binoculars, pointing out a favourite. We watch a shoveler duck sleep in the reeds, a lapwing strut back and forth over its island and two cormorants fight over what turns out to be an eel. Its long litheness slips between the cormorants until one, victorious, swallows it whole. But it makes heavy weather of it, only seeming to realize what it has got itself into halfway through its elongated meal. With one last, enormous effort, it pushes it down, then looks so pleased with itself that we can't help laughing.

Altogether we see black-headed gulls, Canada geese, gadwalls, great black-backed gulls, greylag geese, coots, cormorants, lapwings, little grebes, mallards, Mediterranean gulls, moorhens, oystercatchers, reed warblers, sand martins, shoveler ducks and tufted ducks. I can tell it's going to be difficult, in my visiting of wetlands, to keep a focus on the ground when so much is in the air and in the water.

In the muddy bank, spindly-legged avocets balance and I think, suddenly, of the flamingos I saw with my father in Kenya, as a child. There is a symmetry of shapes over the years, continents and species, as the images superimpose, one on top of the other. I try to remember where exactly we'd seen them – Lake Nakuru, Lake Baringo – I run through old words not used for decades before landing on the right one: Naivasha.

Louise hands me her binoculars to see a little ringed plover. From this little, shuffling bird, my eyes move up to black-headed gulls in the wind, backing up on themselves, careening, gathering momentum before swooping, stalling, swooping, stalling. I continue to watch until I forget where I am, forget everything I think I know about myself. Time moves so slowly that it is like a dreamscape we have entered. It is not the painstaking, absorbing slowness of moss time but little moments of suspension, bubbles of time that envelope you, carrying you for a while before bursting into the present.

RIVER DERWENT

I shape paper into segments, making packets for moss samples. Although I know I'm unlikely to use them, I enjoy this meditative time, when the repetitive action gives a moment of mindfulness. But today, they are chaotically folded – all soaring ridges and pits to fall through – and, oh, the hard-edged thrill of them! I give it up for a lost cause and try some balancing yoga poses instead. I keep falling out of them. Whatever is moving through me today is electric. It is both a de-centring and re-forming. And becoming something else is disorientating. As I travel towards the river and to M on this spring bank holiday, I become aware of my face folding into a ridge of joy. Smiling suddenly feels so incongruous. Why should joy erupt from the body in this particular curve? Why is the body so suddenly peculiar?

'Wren, grey wagtail, blackcap, song thrush,' the bird names fall off M's lips like water as we circle each other, concentric rings on the river, oscillating.

'Goldfinch, goosander ducklings.' There is an acrocarp I don't know, singing a loud lime in amongst the Marilyn moss with spiked sporophytes and a brown and white snail shell. I am drawn to the density of textures. As the deep water flows by, M stands at a slight distance. I become interested in the spaces between us.

'Buzzard calling. Up in that tree,' he says. Birding forms a large part of his days. Like his favourite waders, he is rarely far from the

water and seems to carry some of its qualities. Loose and flowing
in all he does, effortlessly, he sweeps me up. Not with the force of
a torrent but the bounce of a running brook. A cormorant flows
up-river with its low, black beating. I glimpse a clutch of Glowflake, spindly with age, and handle it fondly. 'This is my favourite
moss,' I tell him. A dense spread of Marilyn along a fallen tree
by the bank reminds me of the mosses gathered from Cave Valley for my moss shoes. I like to get down low, where it is warmer
and more still, like the mosses themselves, growing in the boundary layer. I squat by the water's edge as M draws near, hovers.
The energy shifts between us as an egret flaps over the river like a
handkerchief. It feels like a different texture to my days. It feels like
something branching.

We watch a great crested grebe, with its jaunty feathers. M runs
his hand through chestnut hair, ruffling his plumage.

'Sedge warbler, Cetti's warbler,' he ripples on. A kingfisher
flashes us out of our postures. This one is so orange and large it is
a salmon, leaping over. It flits, incandescent, up-river. 'I'm going to
scope that mud bank,' M announces, lifting his telescope onto his
shoulder in one swift scoop. He has almost reached his destination
before I realize he has gone. There is no procrastination, no room
for brooding. He is all fluid movement.

Caught in his slipstream, I, too, take off, drawn by big clumps
of Kind Spears with glowing red sporophytes. The clumps are
so chunky it is like a glacial landscape, a mossy moon landing,
entwined with tails of *Isothecium alopecuroides* – Marilyn's relative, Larger Mouse-tail Moss. I follow the swirling leaves that seem
to wash through with ease. Tufts of moss, hillocks, breasts make a
wholly fertile moment, as I linger over the sporophytes.

It takes another kingfisher to jolt us back together. We follow
the sparkling, turquoise trill of it. Egret after egret, white after
white wash over a waterfall. White garlic, white cloud, white foam,
white bird. There is an easy billowing, a free-fall of colour running between us. A third kingfisher passes. They make, the three

together, a little flotilla of joy, a bright flash of life as it is now, fledging with light and filled with flight.

Further downriver, I see my first swallows of the year. I have been waiting for this moment for weeks. The first soaring uplift of that white underbelly and those lithe wings. I ask M what the collective noun for swallows is. He reels off a list of possibilities from which I choose 'richness'. A richness of swallows. 'Yes, that's lovely,' he agrees. As they drift off over the water, the river is swollen with loveliness. I draw up a silent inventory of our collisions – arm brush, cheek touch, skin blush – as the white throbbing overhead swoops and loops between us, a secret speech of wild, incoming intimacy.

RAMPANT HAPPINESS
Isothecium alopecuroides, Larger Mouse-tail Moss

A-swirl, a-whirl, a leafy twirl, you hold such movement in each curl – to be still yet always moving, to be fixed yet full of music, pure enthusiasm running through each leafy spasm. Your Latin name, *Isothecium*, refers to just this balance – how you have a symmetry that guides the way you manage every aspect of your life, even when things don't go right. You have resources you can draw on that lighten and perform a fluid action. Your attraction is your easy-going flow that doesn't dampen, it's as though you're rampant with happiness.

And when you're touched, you emit heat. And when you're left, you don't deplete. You carry on, you're always moving, it's a rhythm so alluring everybody has to follow, even the hollow find a heart when this moss begins its dance. I don't know where laughter starts. Is it what's left when all else goes? Or is there nothing else for those, like you, who are naturally buoyant? You tell me not to destroy it with questions. Enjoy it. You tell me not to destroy it with questions. Enjoy it.

MIDDLETON LAKES

The sky is piled with humming intricacy. Wilting leaf and sweet balm, starling bursts and swift-swerves over sweeping shoveler ducks. The Middleton Lakes Reserve in the River Tame valley is not far from our Birmingham homes and Louise and I make it over for a few hours. Wind flicks through the rushes with an endless shuffling of things not coming to rest, as two swans pass where I stand at the water's edge. They extend their necks, breaking the surface at exactly the same moment each time, in a kind of watery apple bobbing. I stand and wait for them to pass, knowing it would be wrong to interrupt or in any way alter this practised intimacy. Uniquely choreographed, they slide through the last of the sun that catches at the butterwort, tickles the oystercatcher, coots and flat stretches of liquid glass.

Above, is a busy flightpath of black-headed gulls beneath cormorants, beneath swallows, beneath an airplane. But the sky is altogether separate from the swans, from their cool slippage in complete, absorbed unison. 'Unwearied still, lover by lover / They paddle in the cold' (ll. 19–20) – in his poem 'The Wild Swans at Coole', Yeats was fearful of the moment he would find they had flown away.[7] I wonder how M feels when the birds leave. I've only ever seen him all enthusiasm for their arrival. I wonder what part of him goes when they do.

When I ask him, some days later, he is nonchalant. 'There's never an end to the birding,' he replies. I press him. Surely there is an absence that matches the fullness of their presence? Surely there is, sometimes, a sense of loss? 'Well, when you see a lot of flocking hirundines and realize they're about to embark on a potentially hazardous journey, perhaps,' he concedes. 'But then it's nice to see a swift still around in September or a ring ouzel still in the hills in October.' There really isn't much sadness to the conversation. No shadow of a loss not talked of. M seems to have filled himself so fully with the joy that loss is a strange phenomenon I have to explain to him. He looks at it from a distance, like he's aware of it but it means little to him. I contemplate what it must be like to live so far removed from sadness. To look at it so distractedly, not square in the face, as befits something that could tear you apart whole, but while actively thinking of something else, not believing that it merits your full attention.

CORS DYFI

This wetland reserve of bog, scrub, swamp and wet woodland in Powys in mid-Wales is where Louise visits the osprey, and, this time, I come with her. From the observatory, we view a large female in the nest, making short work of a mullet. Her head seems big, although proportionate to the rest of her body, and her eyes, huge within it. I am drawn to the variations in scale. From the tiny moss in the bog that cannot yet be seen, to the pennywort growing higher and the rising reeds, to the shrub, to the silver birch, the willow and up to the osprey tower and – through the telescope – the nest, and the eyes, expansive in the magnified head, to the hills behind, flanking the sky and through the webcam, out, in a digital sea, through eyes wider than any human geography.

From these dizzying heights, we climb down and out into bog. By the boardwalk, we see common lizards dart in and out of the reeds and emperor dragonflies basking on leaves. We find our favourite plants: bog myrtle, cotton grass and rosebay willowherb. And I, at last, can see the moss: *Sphagnum papillosum*, its branches splayed like starfish. I squat to follow its course amongst the reeds, rising, at length, to a sharp shock.

'Don't look now,' I say, quietly. 'But there's a buffalo over there.'

'Oh, they're the water buffalo!' Louise beams. 'They're here over the summer.' The buffalo are welcomed here for their grazing and the sight of them sparks a memory of Masai Mara Game Reserve in Kenya, and how, as a child, I had visited with my father.

There had been huge packs of buffalo, then, who would take off and charge, spilling like ink over dry land.

Then, the insistent call of a reed warbler brings me back – and the lower-down chime of a grasshopper. Mellowed by the living breath of our surroundings, our thoughts turn to gin. A local company, the Dyfi Distillery, produces drinks using locally foraged botanicals, among them our beloved bog myrtle, pine tips, gorse flower, heather, birch and bramble. We breathe in the deep sweetness of the myrtle as it ripples in over the reed beds.

'We can serve Dyfi gin at our Bog Discos,' we concur. Somewhere in between the soundtracks of our trips to the bogs – Motown, house and vintage Kylie – and the seemingly endless stream of wedding discos we have found ourselves unwitting participants in when stopping at a particular pub on our way home, lies the concept of the Bog Disco. The invitation of the wide-open skies over the bogs also seems to speak of dancing, gatherings and swathes of lifting bodies, you have to pick your feet up high to move through moss – you dance, not walk, through a bog.

STARFISH

Sphagnum papillosum, Papillose Bog-moss

Pillows for elbows pillows for ribs pillows for kneecaps pillows for hips
pillows for eyebrows pillows for teeth pillows for every part underneath
the skin the intestine the bladder and brain pillows for the starfish living
in the veins pillows for baskets made of pillow twigs pillows for the brittle
unfinished and split pillows for nostrils pillows for gums pillows for earlobes
pillows for tongues say everything in pillow that needs to be undone,
spread your constellations when the work is done.

HAM WALL

I trudge along through the fog. The rain has been falling for hours, which means it feels like it has been falling for months, which means, or so it seems to the body, that there has never been anything but rainfall, nothing, ever, but this soaked chill, this wet-whipped, sodden grip. On this short trip from Birmingham, there wasn't time to wait for the weather to change. Now, I walk the threads of water, long and thin and straight, a landscape not meant for my thoughts, which are wider and looser and more in line, or circle, with the bogs that squelch at the edges.

Every now and then I feel that my phone is vibrating, though I know I have it switched off. I keep checking. Nothing. If it is not my phone, then it is someone blowing over a pan-pipe. I scan and re-scan the reed beds. Some honking from the bank to the left draws me in. I squat at the edge. All grows silent, except for a helicopter, pulsing overhead. I don't know what it is searching for, I wonder if it is me, at the precarious tip of reed edge, a hair's breadth from the water.

I wait, lulled by the calls of ducks, now familiar. There is breathing in the reeds before me. There is the in and out of air over the windpipes of more-than-human lives ahead of me. There is a steady exhale of sound that has nothing to do with me, from a body with nothing to do with me, for a life that has nothing to do with me, and, yet – I feel so connected to this eerie exhalation that I stay here, wet to the bone, toes frozen, chest tightening, at the soggy water's edge, waiting, just for the chance to meet it, just for the chance to see whose lungs are these.

A tawny muzzle in the reeds. A nudging of feathers. A bittern. Its plumage so precisely matches the reeds, which so precisely match my skin, that there is a bonding in the field of colour. I don't move. I will not enter anything hostile into this moment. I will not let my humanness let me down. We beat together; one, two, three.

Dark eye to dark eye. One, two, three. There is fear here but I am learning what to do with that now. I have learned that the body will want to go to the worst possible outcome but that if you can hold it here, at its tipping point, sit inside this in-between-ness, you can give it the time it needs to consider if it wouldn't, in fact, rather go somewhere else. The bittern beats. One, two, three. I channel what I know of ease. As it makes its retreat, time begins again.

WICKEN FEN

I slip through the fens and Olly, the RSPB's Senior Climate Change Policy Officer, meets me off the train. We make our way to Wicken Fen Reserve, nine miles south of Ely, home to over 9,000 species, including some of the rarest and most endangered. Every now and then, I stand still and stare for no obvious reason, while he moves with pace and purpose. At one stationary point, he asks me what I'm doing.

I find it hard to articulate what pulls me in to a particular place, or, once the initial attraction has occurred, what I do with it. I often won't know in advance what will happen and that waiting and stillness are part of the process. He tells me how he recently read an interview about a cyclist who thought of the hobby as not 'wasting' time but 'making' time. Is my practice a making of time, he asks? It feels more like a tuning in to different kinds of time that are already in motion, I say. Like the slowness of moss, or soil, or the deep accumulations of peat.

I ask him about the role of peatlands and the importance of mosses. He explains how mosses are valuable for long-term carbon storage but that there is also a need for more immediate action, and for this, there is nothing to rival trees, although even they take a few years to mature from planted saplings or whips to being useful carbon sinks and must be planted in the right place and not in peat soils. This durational point is an important one – it can take a hundred years for one metre of peat to form. However, it is also vital that the carbon sinks of peat bogs do not become carbon sources, emitting carbon when degraded. Peatlands are the world's largest terrestrial organic carbon stock and that needs to stay in the ground, not enter the atmosphere in harmful greenhouse gases.

We watch a reed warbler flit in and out of the reeds. Staring into the bed requires a deep level of absorption. I don't know if I'm bored or at peace, it feels like a place between emotions, a flattening and suctioning. Deep stillness, punctuated by little pockets of birdsong. The National Trust calls this place 'a window on a "lost landscape"', referring to the undrained fenland which was once such a feature of these lowlands. As I drift into these lost lands, Olly's voice flits over, describing how peatlands used to be designated as wastelands on maps. Wildernesses. And while it can, for a moment, feel that way – the uniform beige grass, the flatness of water – as the eye trains, it lights, everywhere, on difference; the flash of fen violets, the sparkling milk parsley, the tantalizing glint of the recoverable.

'I've lost all sense of time,' I tell Olly.

'Good,' he replies.

WICKEN LODE

Under heavy skies, we move off the reserve to walk along the lode. A canal boat heaves past, leaving a slick of oil in the water we had been considering entering. 'What do you think?' he asks. I'm not quite as ready to go under these days. I carry an injury now which means my spine may spasm for days after hitting cold water. The tension gathers between my shoulders and takes up residence. My body holds all sorts of inhabitants it never used to.

'Doubtful,' I reply.

'But we've come so far!' he encourages.

'I will if you will,' I concede, and he is straight in, dropping off the reed bed. His head lifts above the water and I watch its rise and fall, steadily growing small as he swims on. When he reaches the bend he looks back, full of exhilaration and packed with the cold rush of the water. I wait until my eyes can no longer register the boat's oil, before following.

My feet find soft mud. Now I know what the swans know, as I nest in the reeds, dreaming a shelter. My feet are wide and webbed as I drift in and out of cover, as the bittern showed me how to at Ham Wall. In the long stretch of the lode, I am lithe and slippery. In the shallow water, I burrow like a water worm, gliding through mud. I am a body touching a body – a silk worm, a slow worm, a slip worm, a slick worm – in the lode I have swum, I have flowed, I have sewn and been stitched, I have slipped myself in.

Olly swims toward me and we float, for a moment, suspended. Stretching the skin as the light lifts, spreading the limbs like starfish. If the reed warbler above finds anything amiss in our presence, it doesn't show it, bobbing from blade to blade.

I shiver. As I adjust to the world of air and uprightness, body shrugging back to its usual fit, I hover. As, for a while, things stay with us – a different posture, expanded lungs, tendrils of hair, strange sheens over land the eyes forgot, things seen that to others stay lost. We are wanderers. Seafarers. Back from distant lands, from wilderness. I start to edge across. From wasteland to wetland is a slip of letters, a trickle of time. Olly hands me his coffee and I warm through. I shine.

6. SUNDIAL

ROUDSEA WOODS

I shine. Bright, against the pine, drawing closer to the mosses. There are strange sheens over the land I edge across. Together with the other bog enthusiasts from a nearby conference on restoring lowland raised peat bogs in Cumbria, we are wanderers, seafarers – but, soon, I am cut off. Back in the world of air and uprightness, my thoughts are interrupted by practical points about the restoration process. When the peat bogs are healthy and waterlogged, they create a carbon sink so effective that some believe they could be the key to geoengineering a cooler climate. But when the peat is drained or burned, the balance needed for safe carbon storage is disturbed and hundreds of years of stored carbon can be released into the atmosphere. Amid the immediacy of these practical concerns, there is no moment of quiet. There is no space to stop and wait for the moss.

Someone hands me a head of *Sphagnum capillifolium* and tells me it's a Sphagnum. I have learned a great deal from the scientists – what Sphagnum mosses look like, their relationship to peat, how and why to restore a peat bog – but this gift seems superfluous, like me handing back a Shakespeare sonnet and saying, *It's a poem*. I accept it, but press it back down among the mosses moments later. The exchange is well-meaning but what more could we be sharing here, the scientists and poets?

BUD

Sphagnum capillifolium, Acute-leaved Bog-moss

Burrow and blow,
furrow and flow along
peat, splinter and piece leaf by leaf
the belief that the body will grow, the relief
to have something to show for that time spent
huddled below surface. You earned this
from such heavy, lengthy lessons
in inflorescence.

I straggle at the back, waiting for a chance to dip my fingers into the sunny bog water, undetected. I don't know what I'm looking for, only that it takes silence and listening to respond to the glistening.

When the time comes, it is thrilling. There is something exhilarating about the unusual orange-coloured water and its unexpected heat, as I dangle my fingers through. Brushed with moss, my skin basks in the liquid sun. Seeing moss not chiefly as something to observe but as a being, a collection of beings, that you might come – somehow, and however incompletely – to know, means there is a deep joy in drawing close. Even without knowledge of their processes, it is enlivening to come up against their edges, feel the brush of their branches, the glow of their leaves, the pull of their rhythms and sparkling wreaths. Yet, when you know, too, how they are keeping carbon from entering the atmosphere as a harmful greenhouse gas, the connection becomes deeper, more integral than that – it is something like homage, or the keeping of a promise. In goes the whole hand, the wrist, a stretch of the arm. But soon I will be missed and must return to the group. I pull up, reluctantly, shaking myself loose.

BLACK BOG

I land down, tentatively, placing my boots flush against soft rush. Northern Ireland is home to a quarter of the UK's active raised bogs and I have travelled west from Cumbria to visit one of the largest active lowland raised bogs in the country: Black Bog in County Tyrone. When Ballynahone Bog, the second-largest intact lowland raised bog in the country, had been threatened with cutting for horticultural peat, a conservation campaign featuring a slogan from the Ulster Wildlife Trust inviting people to 'take their last walk on an Ulster bog' had helped to safeguard the site as an Area of Special Scientific Interest. I think of all the feet to tread the bog before, of a future where we may no longer be able to access what it stores.

Ecologist Trish Fox has been working to conserve Black Bog, conducting surveys which show the condition of the bog declining. During her work here, Trish has pieced together many stories of how the people and bog have interacted over time. She speaks of pools in the bog stretching 15 feet deep, seagulls nesting and black-headed gulls. She reveals how many living there have told her that it used to be a lough – while this is how many bogs form, it is a very slow process, taking place over thousands of years.

'I interpreted this as a sort of living memory passed down by many generations,' she explains. Unlike the digital hive minds connected by cable, there are bog minds that work through plant-human fable – memories interleaved, waiting to be woken. And as the carbon the mosses are storing makes them custodians, holding onto what would threaten others, I wonder if we might find stored in us an ability to protect others from harm. Could we house an empathetic vision held under the skin, connecting us to other forms of living?

WOOL WI-FI

Sphagnum fallax, Flat-topped Bog-moss

Rootless roots, wireless wires,
spreading underneath with fire green and simmering
with snow, crushing in between the toes, a light leaf-fall that dusts
and winnows, a shoal of shining, threaded minnows, flashing in between the nodes,
climbing deep, transmitting slow, following each old advance in this technology
of plants, an ancient, woven, wet, ditch-dance, where anyone can take a turn,
swerving into future gladly, merging into selfhood madly, raucous grace
and balanced glee at being what you're meant to be, knotted
in an ancestry of kindness knitted in the reeds.

Trish tells me about her work with Sphagnum mosses and how she has been trained in a Canadian method of Sphagnum relocation that has been used on an industrial scale in Canada following the removal of peat for horticulture. She also explores other methods of Sphagnum reintroduction, like plug planting. I ask if she has a favourite moss.

'Well, I think I do.' She reveals a picture of *Sphagnum fuscum* – Rusty Bog-moss, its orange leaves spreading sunshine through. 'I suspect I like this one because, like *Sphagnum austinii*, it is so recognizable in the field.' As she speaks about how difficult Sphagnum is to identify, I think of my own process of coming by these plants – sometimes a strict routine of lens and key, other times a touch, a feeling of the air between us, a sharing of the ground that weaves us.

GINGER SPICE

Sphagnum fuscum, Rusty Bog-moss

Crackle of shoots, pheasant's roost,
sun flushing over the hummocks
a ginger, a peach, a flummox of oranges
peeling, that flourishing feeling, to be
brought to life again by the spice
in a stem, to be called to earth again
by a flash in the fen, autumn colours
fusing, burnished bracken moving on
a blackened spine, polishing the rind.

This is the furthest distance that my moss journeys have taken me so far. I am even more careful not to take any moss away, since I don't know if I will be coming again and whether I will be able to return it. I ask myself if this makes the landscape less 'mine', as I cannot take a piece away – or more, since I need a map stored inwardly, to preserve enough of it in me. As long working hours have told on the body, I am thankful that it could bring me this far and try hard to steady the ragged beat of the breath. If a bog is 'wasted' land, not bound by utility, I think – if we cannot rest here, then where can we?

The long-entrenched view of the bog as wasted land is also, here, bound up with the land appropriation of past English drain-ing projects that sought to make the land more profitable. As I lower to the sun-drenched mosses, I think of the bog bodies pre-served for thousands of years in the peat. When unearthed, some have become symbols of the violence of anti-colonial struggles, through the marks of historic violence found on them. Seamus Heaney has drawn parallels between what has come to the surface in bogs and the violence surfacing in Northern Ireland. Emblems such as Heaney's ravaged Bog Queen are powerfully affective, yet, as I reach the bog and sit, I am conscious of not wishing to be assim-ilated into it. I am no myth, nor otherly creature, though have as much right to be here on these grounds of plant companionship and pleasure as for any more appropriating endeavour.

I turn onto my back. Streaming, speeding between violet and red, between visible and felt, at lower levels than the eye detects, here, at ground state – I stretch. I absorb, I let go of, I travel in the slow earth. I am only available in moments. My preferred state is inertness. I relax back down to the spread of the leaf in the low-locked flood where everything heats, loosening knots, undo-ing pleats, immersed in bronze water – I reach. There are stored in me deep reserves of resonance, throbbing with worlds that take up residence if the body opens fully. Between hummock and hollow pool, between shoulder blades and the spool of the spine unthread-ing, here in the lough I am treading. Held by the pelvis like a buoy, between the peat and mineral soil, energy shoots along limbs, branches for ribs, in wet rims of skin.

SOUTH PENNINES

Inlets stream in where I spring on the surface of Stanbury Moor. On my way back down the country, I have come to the moorlands known to the Brontës. Top Withens Farm is thought to be the location of Wuthering Heights, and Penistone Crag the outcrop of gritstone that Emily Brontë describes as a meeting place for Heathcliff and Cathy. As the water trickles through my toes, there is a stirring from the quiet stones.

The upland moors of West Yorkshire are important carbon stores, and a small local area, as indicated on maps showing carbon- and nature-rich areas released by the RSPB to mark World Environment Day on 5 June 2019, holds a million tonnes. To prevent harmful levels of carbon-dioxide emissions, there is a need to watch what rises from the ground, to bring succour to those captured in the drought. Peat re-wetting can prevent carbon release and make the peatland less susceptible to the fires that would release even higher amounts of carbon, destroying organic material that has taken thousands of years to form.

Brontë knew what it is to be thoroughly saturated, showing 'Cathy . . . standing bonnetless and shawl-less to catch as much water as she could with her hair and clothes', and Heathcliff, who, although one 'could not think him dead . . . his face and throat were washed with rain; the bed-clothes dripped, and he was perfectly still'.[8] With my feet soaking in the wetness, I think of the swans from Middleton Lakes, sliding through water in choreographed unison. I think of Cathy and Heathcliff, after death, submerged yet thought to be strewn again among the air – its ghostly heirs. Asleep, but their hearts awake; dead but with nectar drenched, since they are together now, since they have survived the drought.

I take little bounces. Through heather and moss, my skin lifts and drops. I remember how Lockwood, the tenant of neighbouring Thrushcross Grange, after learning of Cathy and Heathcliff's deaths, 'lingered round them . . . and wondered how any one could ever imagine unquiet slumbers for the sleepers in that quiet earth'.[9] Heels nudge onto stem, resting. Toes tinge with heat, through bright netting. I may not see my father now, yet, there are senses which allow our contact, that expand and contract – though dormant for days, when re-wetted are glazed – brushed by skin and filtered into a place where peat, once lost, is cresting, where in loss life is pressing. I feel the membranes thinning, a slipway of skin doused and spinning.

LLYN TRAWSFYNYDD

At midday, off Llyn Trawsfynydd, two rainbows bounce and glisten. When Louise and I make it to Wales, we find summer has already arrived as we move off-road, following gold. With the longer light we can cover more ground, and, while the city mosses have brought comfort each day, it is a special pleasure to feel concrete give way to something soft, to the pull of the bog.

Before the lake was constructed here in Gwynnedd in North Wales, the area was part of a marshland known as Gors Goch and somewhere nearby is, according to Louise, a 'a secret bog'. We follow our coveted co-ordinates over ground that is rarely trodden. It is tough going, as we haul our legs high over long grass, only to have them plummet down into copper water, then deeper and darker into peat. The moss grows in hummocks here, in a sequence of hilltops. We bounce from hillock to hillock as though part of a mossy moon-landing.

The Sphagnum forms a familiar sequence of Bud (*Sphagnum capillifolium*) mounds. I point out some of the other mosses, telling Louise my name for *Rhytidiadelphus loreus* – 'Tiny Dancer', on account of the way its leaves twist and turn as if in the midst of some hidden musical motion.

TINY DANCER

Rhytidiadelphus loreus, Little Shaggy-moss

Red-green baby, woodland lady
seamstress for the land.
Ballerina, you must have seen her
dancing in the ground.
Come closer, tiny dancer
threading light along the way
lay down amid the grasses
you had a busy day today.

Bending low between the mounds, there is a rush of peach in bursts of leaves. I think of *Sphagnum palustre*, but still need to key it out. Further on, new pastel colours increase. There is such vibrancy, pulling me in. As I listen, I drink; the water and the colour sift through in a kind of filtering. In comes the particular light of the moss, out flows the willingness to see it. Inhale of peach, exhale of welcome. A correspondence travels through us. *Come in*, little peach, soft newness!

Sphagnum pulchrum translates from the Latin as 'beautiful moss' and has the common name, Golden Bog-moss. The field guides suggest so many colours that it might be, that it is difficult to imagine how to identify it. Do you look for orange, or chestnut, or golden or green? But when you see it in the field, all becomes clear. As a sunset may be pink or golden or grey, though you would not mistake it for anything but a sunset, so this moss radiates.

SUNDIAL

Sphagnum pulchrum, Golden Bog-moss.

Yours is the day and yours is the night,
you have made all that ever was made of the light,
there at the boundary of earth and unearth,
summer on summer of seedless birth.
Suns spiralling through dark,
deep dwelling place of our hearts
cresting and falling in peat, to a golden beat.

Before the word beauty, with its French origins, was the Old English word *'wlite'*. Denoting a brightness or splendour in appearance, the word was related to *'wlītan'* – to see, or look at. The act of looking was then itself bound up in beauty. I am careful how I look at moss now, hardly ever dismantling it to view under a lens, taking more comfort from not identifying it than from having to break it in order to do so. *'Wlite,'* I whisper to the moss. *Wlite*. But this is a Welsh moss. Will its rhizoids know the roots I speak with?

Days later, the clipped body of a Bud (*Sphagnum capillifolium*) in a moss packet, the one sample besides the moss-shoe mosses that I have, has lost its vibrancy – just a tinge of red at the head. I douse it in water and wait for the miracle. For when water is added to a moss that has been picked – days, months, even years later, it restores it. The colour spreads from the top, all along its stem, taking in the branch leaves. It is like watching life return to a body – which we did, every time my father fell unconscious – before the slow flushing.

And just like that, I am back under attack. A grief without neutrality, just clashing ferocity, arrives each time as if anew. Always, at the memory of loss, the sun seems to dangle from a string in front of you – this is what you could have had, this dazzle – back and forth, your lost sun swings like a pendulum. I think of my past acts of trespass – using a scalpel to dissect moss for a slide, tearing moss from rocks on the hillside and how I have tried to make my viewing a softer kind of doing. Might it work for mourning too? To still look but with some temperance, in mellowing remembrance, so that grief might appear without ferocity, to bounce over the head like a bubble, to rise like a sun from your rubble.

CORS FOCHNO

Leaf-high, stems flung in a huddle, I slip into treacle water. Feet dipping bronze, the living moss shines before me. It is so full of its green, the *Sphagnum cuspidatum* I have never seen so thoroughly immersed, so that it is part of the water, has made water a springing, fluffy material. The live tips on top, the dead roots below – Sphagnum makes a mockery of what we know of death, showing how to live in both states at once – death and life in easy equilibrium.

Here, north of Aberystwyth on the estuary of the River Dyfi, is one of the most intact lowland raised bogs in Wales and England. The bog has been trapping carbon dioxide from the atmosphere here, accumulating peat, since the last ice age. At first, the smell is of summer and denseness – thick blankets of mosses wrapping over dragonflies and reed beds. Here and there, the mosses cover stumps of oak not yet broken into bog. I press my fingers down and down, following the bodies of the mosses before they are peat. As I pull up a thread, the rotting smell of death-in-life slips out between stained fingers, slicks up the arms, circles the shoulders before settling still in the nostrils.

This is not like other bodies of water, where there is motion. Here there is no current, no sway of wind over water. The Sphagnum fans out leaves as hair, fully saturated, sucking everything in. It is a place of deep peace and sunken security. There is safety deposited in the depth of ground, in the slow suction of peat. This is a place to hold and be held, a still point in a world of motion – a fixed collection of points, of moss heads, anchoring moments.

While we know that carbon loss from this peat would accelerate climate change, the effects of rising temperatures on the peat are not yet conclusive and a project on another part of the bog, the Cors Fochno experiment, aims to simulate the conditions expected under future climates to see how the carbon store is affected. It has already reported White Beak Sedge encroaching on the Sphagnum. With less Sphagnum, there will be less peat and less ability to lock away carbon. There are, everywhere, reasons to sharpen our attention to these mosses and to try to mitigate such losses.

Further in and over the moss carpet, I feel the soft pulse of moss tops, their slow squelch and quiet give. I want to listen to how they live – draw closer still until skin sieves the glowing data. Deeper, bronze water seeps bright over calf, illuminating skin in a tangle of oranges. I grow bolder. Fixing one foot in the shallow moss, I feel I can't get into too much trouble if I fling the other further out. Like the points of a compass drawing a circle, one leg remains rooted while the other pivots into peat. But as I look out to the still sheet of dark water, I know I must leave the safety of the shallow leg. I lift it up and out, one foot after the other, up and out, into darkness.

I squelch down, further each time, submerged. The water is past my knees now and my heart beats with some internal knowing of what is to come. The darkest water swills around my thighs and my heart screams. Whatever part of me that wants to lurch forward to swim is silenced by the part that wants to live. But when I try to lift my legs in retreat, I find that I can't. What had moved so softly into water is now stuck fast. I feel the dark water as a siren, all encouragement up until the point where I couldn't retreat even if I wanted to. I strain and strain, with the furious intensity of swimming when too far out against a strong current. But the peat pulls in another direction, down and down, it won't give me up.

The part of me that doesn't want to leave is fascinated now, by the beauty of bronze water over bronze skin, by what I have become – this water being, peatling. But the greater part, the survivor, heaves itself up and out, up and out, until I am back on the soft carpet of rose-lit moss, until I am on reeds, on fern, on the swaying, seeded grass, billowing and willowing onto land.

THE BOG OF EDEN

Following the river around, we search for a bog by the River Eden in north-west Wales. Passing through woodland, we pick up pine branches to help navigate the terrain. Mine is wonderfully shaped,

SUNDIAL

curved over at the top into a perfect walking stick handle, and I
adopt it as my Bog Stick. Louise's is less reliable and she plunges
down in front of me. Her fair hair splays out as she squelches
through the sludge. Doing our mossy moon-landing dance, legs
hauled high over grass, whole bodies tense with unexpected land-
ings, she turns to ask, 'Do you think we're totally mad?' I pause.

'You know – I suspect that we are.' I come down heavily into a
golden spray of water. 'But I don't think it matters.'

We make it through to a patch of bog myrtle, common butterwort and tousled Sphagnum, with high hills rolling all around.
'This is it,' Louise says, looking up from her map. It's a bit of an
anticlimax. The Bog of Eden should be deep and dark and bur-
densome, or golden and seductively glimmering. Instead, we hadn't
even realized we'd been walking through it. After a while, drifting
between the odd moss hillock, tall grass and heather, I notice my
breath deepening and pulling up from the pit of the belly rather
than the shallow surface of the lungs. I feel the lure of lowering.

Lying back onto bog myrtle, soft clouds of Sphagnum below,
white puffs of air above, the sweetness pours in. Wrapped up in
the sweetness is a healing. It is not only the Sphagnum's carbon
storing that repairs but its wound-dressing properties too. The
myrtle's antiseptic qualities pump as I press the leaf gently through
my thumb and forefinger, rolling, to release the scent. There is
a swift release of perfume and light as the sun breaks out from
behind my fingers. I rise from the ground in slow increments of
spine, so that first I see the top of the bog myrtle, then the heads
of the grass, then the ferns in the field and hills beyond. Seated,
my sitting bones press down into Sphagnum, anchored in water.
I feel like a water lily, or an extension of the Sphagnum, as the
water seeps through.

I continue up from my seated position and plant my hands
down into wet moss. Stretching my legs behind me, I hover in
Plank position. Pushing back into heels and lifting, I lever into
Downward Dog, having drifted into Bog Yoga. In this arched pose,

nose brushing Sphagnum, hands sinking lower into water, I feel a humble tucking of the body and move with the small, slow pull of moss. Low in the ground, arms elbow-deep in bog, I push the chest forward and up with the sphinx-like rise of Cobra pose. The lift of head over myrtle, the full spread of the shoulders, the feeling of rising fully from moss into hill seems to come from a place of neat strength. This is what I can do with the body – the will, the mind, the core, the guts. If this will to rise comes from a snake, it is not the seducer from the Garden but the Cobra from the Bog. As I lift full body up from ground, bubbles of laughter spill. I approach Louise, smiling.

'I've been doing Bog Yoga.'

'I couldn't see you – I thought you'd disappeared.' So much has sunk into the peat but I have risen with a gentle heat – a microscopic sun, I beat.

BORTH

At a touch, it could retreat – the battered coast between Borth and Ynyslas in mid-Wales. Waves churning, sky burning with pressurized clouds, these are the last moments before the rain comes, pitching the sea to a higher ferocity. I veer in towards the tree stumps swathed in seaweed that perforate the coastline. Their green trails seem to lengthen, extending down and up, pulling my eyes along with them. In a matter of moments, I am walking into green, through the forest that was here thousands of years ago. The stumps I come to start to rise, to lengthen into towering oaks, ending in a vast leaf canopy. The closer I get to the trees, the more their scale increases until I feel, even as I stand on sand, that I am in dense woodland, surrounded and enclosed, in spite of open sea in front of me. The ease with which I get there is striking. Like a lens cap flipping off binoculars, I am suddenly seeing, have switched, effortlessly, into forest eyes.

This forest is usually hidden by a layer of sand, only exposed under particular climactic circumstances. Recent storms have shaken up the ground, dislodging sand to reveal the flattened peat with its hoard of roots of ancient alder, birch, oak and pine. The forest's existence seems a double secret – hidden under sea at high tide, hidden under sand except on the rare occasions when chance intervenes. The wide berths of the trees tell of their age – 6,000-year-old radii. The wood is soft to touch, weathered by sea and sand and peat and death, wearing away into pulp, dotted with glittering strips of seaweed. As I touch it, the sea swirls in, reminding me that this connection is only temporary, that I haven't long before it is taken.

This forest growing out of sea, with no division between the elements, shouldn't be possible. Yet, here it is. An impossibility clearly visible, made manifest. And that is what a wetland is. Land growing out of water, water made of land. A 'wetland' is a portmanteau that takes apart binary thinking; not wetness and a separate land but wetness and land in and of each other. Forest that is sea, sea that is forest. And I think of all the possible impossibilities that wash in and out of focus; how dependent they are on where and how we look.

OFF-GRID

Dense leaves entwine and hook the toes in golden water. Humps of reeds are friends, providing anchors. I move forwards as Louise scouts either side of the path. Always it is an assessment – how far down will I go, how will I get back up? I step further into Sphagnum. First, the darker green, then the lighter Sphagnum 'soup', then the peach-coloured knots, tightly bound like fishing nets. I have rolled my leggings up and am knee-deep.

'People,' Louise calls. I squat in the reeds, so low down that I have to bring leggings to Sphagnum, and am soon soaked through.

As I wait, my heart beats to the clang of their feet. They seem far closer than I know them to be. Perhaps only centimetres. I shiver in the reed beds, thinking of the hunted birds who have done the same. I recall John Clare's snipe – 'Lover of swamps / The quagmire over grown / With hassock tufts of sedge – where fear encamps / Around thy home alone / The trembling grass / Quakes from the human foot' (ll. 1–6)[10] – I peep up to see they have travelled far into the distance. I'm so wet now, I may as well keep going. I take my leggings off, my top, and wade into water. The knotted Sphagnum breaks my fall as I make my way in. I am used to swimming in cold water but this is excruciating. I go deeper, past white feathers resting on dark-green moss – I wonder who these white remnants of body belonged to, as I cross.

OPHELIA

Sphagnum cuspidatum, Feathery Bog-moss

Submerged, you search for the hidden path, for the brace of stars
that would steer you right – you can't see what I see – how you
ignite the dark, that those searching for light might themselves be
sparks. What if Ophelia had – simply got out – of the water? I see
her everywhere, entering rooms at night with her leaves tipped
white – in despair of the care she needs, unaware of the trail she
leaves.

Looking out to the dark pool, I lurch forwards, not knowing what I am moving into, whether it will treat me softly or entangle me in dangers not yet felt or imagined by the body. For a moment, I think it is the latter. I am tangled and the cold is excruciating, cracking the neck, breaking along the spine, ice splintering the shoulders. My feet are caught, my arms are caught. I am frozen, trapped, and where is breath? But in the next instant, sun falls in off the reed tops, washes across the Sphagnum, onto my face. I lift up from the moss and pull free, gliding a few strokes forward, shrieking with exuberant relief.

Louise is laughing at me from the bank.

'It is SO cold,' I shout.

'People!' Louise cries. Again, I lie, shivering, in my reed-nest, soaking wet, ants and spiders running over me as people pass overhead. They seem to move so slowly. Finally, Louise calls out and I emerge. 'There are more on the way,' she says. It's a rush to dress as I pull clothes on out of sequence: T-shirt inside out, leggings back to front, before re-joining her on the path. And, just like that, I am back in the land of people.

Through Cumbria, Northern Ireland, Yorkshire and Wales, I have waited for, and waded in, mosses for days. From fingertips to shoulder; from the toes, all over. In place of a peat corer an arm. In place of carbon the balm of a new connection held in me. Flooded by moss-sun, I have reached myself out, tingling and tangling in the spread. I have travelled to the borders of our being – skin to leaf, heart to branch – and stored what I am seeing in my cells. The light grows, between us, a swell. Though returned to land, I am not the same, I hold in me a gentle flame. A creeping affinity with the hunted, a gliding, a surge, a beloved entanglement of earth exists if you step just a little off-course. The body freshens through a soft transgression.

7 . LIMELIGHT

*'Perhaps no great group of plants has so few uses, commercial
or economic, as the mosses'*
Henry S. Conrad, How to Know the Mosses and Liverworts

THE RETREAT

The body freshens through a soft transgression. To not always do
what is expected, to take a habit and reject it, can provide a new
path through. *To not have to be liked, to not have to be accomplished, to not have to be beautiful. To not have to speak, to not
have to engage, to not have to be interesting. To be present and
for that to be enough. To not give out and for that to be enough.*
I hear the words spill from me as we take ourselves to the borders
of our being and tell each other what we are seeing. Away from the
spotlight of our public selves, a gentle flame glows in the cells. The
light grows between us, a swell.

Mosses know how to make do with little. Though they lack
roots to store water, they are able to dry out without physiologi-
cal damage, going dormant until the next watering. Growing in
groups increases the surface area available to capture rain, so that
when it comes, it is made the most of. I turn from face to face of
the retreatants – away from the limelight, we start to colour in. We
soak in a radial flush. *We are here and that is enough.*

There is a no-speaking policy before the first session, which, to
me, is a balm. To move without speech is to live without breach, as
we are allowed to continue in our own paths, not cut off or pulled
back by the need to interact. And yet, it is not isolation. There is
still companionship in this slip along the seam of communication.
There is camaraderie in our bodies sharing space, silently charging

together like a bank of grass. It is a rare opportunity to live beyond utility, to see what else being might be.

Later, walking to a nearby waterfall, gentle conversation passes from stranger to stranger. Along the hill ridge, we are only able to move two abreast and our partners change according to our walking speeds – like a country dance, we rotate. As we reach the water's edge, some cool their feet, others sit at a distance. I enter the pool, watching the mosses spread along the rock. There is a furry one I don't yet know, whose leaves I smooth. A woman who has picked up a feather is watching me. She draws near, expectant. 'I just really like mosses,' I explain, lamely. She brightens. 'Oh! What is it about them?' In the woman who picks up feathers and the woman who strokes mosses there is a symmetry. I say something about leaves, about light. I say nothing, yet, of the majesty of their cells under a microscope, or the way they, for me, embody hope. Yet, I see that she catches some of it anyway, whatever is deeply folded in my rapport with mosses is reflected in her face, full of new shine.

I take longer to walk back, lending my attention to the mosses. They take me off-path, as, eyes down, I come to a series of rabbit holes. I think of what the yogi had said to me earlier. She had invited me to let my neck soften, to not hold my spine so tight. *There is more space there than you know, so much further you can go.* I lean into new territory, craning into darkness. With an ocean flowing out of the head, I do not know which way to thread the bones together. Feet are anchored still but there is no knowing what the upward parts will do. I have no idea where I am going. Then, a spark. A sudden soaring of light. I know, before I have keyed it out, or allowed for any formal system of identification, that this is *Schistostega pennata* – Goblin Gold. With a simple structure of threadlike chains of cells, it has a refractive quality that causes a unique luminescence. The unexpected flare of phosphorescence is the sky in a meteor shower, but the sky is the earth and the earth is the depth and the depth is the slip of the skin when it is no longer a covering but a way to let the light in.

I know, in that moment, how little I am qualified to talk about light. I am scrunched up, tightly bound, with weights secreted in the tiniest of places – in fingernails, follicles, underneath the knee-caps. So, for the kind of light that is visible, that flows through you and gladdens the skin, I am simply not sure where to begin. And so much of our sociability depends upon it. There is an artificial light, that can be switched on and off at will – that, I know all about. I can beam at lighthouse levels, hit just the right note to draw the required response. But more and more frequently, I don't. I find myself refusing. There is a battle I am choosing to take on, between ease and pleasing, artifice and leaving the costumes behind that no longer fit. Increasingly, I dream of the half-light, the dusk, the gloaming – where there might only be the smallest illumination but it is true and permeates through the whole being, glowing through the field, the hill, the pavement.

When I look at moss light, I feel my own switching on. We pulse between ourselves, on – on, warmer and lighter. At its brightest in water, after rain, I have watched moss move from earthly light to a constellation. I would like to try those modes too. From earth-light to constellation, without artificial light, with no pollution. And so I find myself shying away, now, from anything needing to be posed. It is either earthlight, or constellation – I know no other modes.

DOROTHY

Schistostega pennata, Goblin Gold

If a beautiful woman falls in a forest with no man around to see, is she still beautiful?

I won't give you a name. No more my place to bestow than yours to receive, you are yourself and I am the briefest of passers-by, and yet – two Dorothies seem to speak through you: Hollywood siren, Hollywood sweetheart – Dorothy Dandridge, Judy Garland.

When Dorothy follows a yellow brick road to an emerald city where every core glows, she could have been walking straight under your leaves, brushing against your neon-lit sleeves. Dorothy Dandridge, however, as you do, knows how it feels to have jewels run through you – to sense you are golden and brilliant and bright, a crystalline vision obscured in plain sight. Accepting her Oscar in 2002, Halle Berry acknowledged a debt paid to you: 'This moment is for Dorothy Dandridge . . . for every nameless, faceless woman of colour that now has a chance because this door tonight has been opened.' I'm hoping. That whoever encounters you understands without question, you are the embodiment of beauty and not the exception.

In *A Treatise Concerning the Principles of Human Knowledge*, George Berkeley suggests, 'there is nothing easier than for me to imagine than trees' but also that 'the objects of sense exist only when they are perceived'. O, glamorous mosses, who thrive no thanks to me, such clamorous gossip has no part in our philosophy. If a luminous moss grows with nobody to see, it is as real as me, it steals the scene.

It was an act of softening that brought me to this moss. If I hadn't let my neck drop, without tensing or trying to force a fixing – if I hadn't let the moorings drift and shift into the unfamiliar configurations of the body – I wouldn't have known the wonder of finding that we are not alone, of seeing that there are others who occupy dark places, without giving in, without dimming. This moss does not perform for me, it is itself and I had the luck to be in its presence – that is true luminescence.

Warming to each other's presence, we settle into our practice. In a different stretch of her life, our yogi starred in the cult series, *Xena: Warrior Princess*. We move through several warrior poses in our hours together but it is Virabhadrasana 1, Warrior Pose 1, that requires the most of me. A vigorous standing pose, it invites you to perform multiple, opposing actions, simultaneously. While lifting up, you push down, and while reaching forward, you stretch back. Within Shaivism, a tradition in Hinduism that reveres the god Shiva, Virabhadra is the fierce warrior who grew out of a lock of Shiva's hair. Shiva had plucked this hair out of his head, distraught, upon learning of the death of his wife, Sati. The warrior Virabhadra, in time, avenges those guilty of contributing towards Sati's death.

Without its usual chemical straightening, my hair begins to fall. For years now, each time the gloop had touched the scalp I had found myself wanting to draw back, yet it takes a while for habits to go, for blocks to break, to re-enter flow. Now, strand after strand, lacking its habitual sustenance, breaks off. At this stage, you can either cut all the previously treated hair off in one bold buzz, or try to retain it while waiting for the new to grow through. If kept, the treated hair needs careful moisturising to minimize breakage. Sometimes I forget. Sometimes, I am too busy pushing forward to remember to look back. I forget the conditioner. I forget to soften.

The hair – at times, the dark pine needles of a forest floor, other times, the wispy trails of a pleurocarp moss – is clear in its signal that it is no longer part of me. I have failed in my duty to keep whole. I think about taking it all off. As I root and lift, in warrior pose, I think of what it is to keep and gift.

The poet, A. Rawlings, once gave her hair away. Warned by doctors that it would fall out, rather than wait passively for that moment she pre-empted it, leaving a long braid of freshly cut hair in a small cave in an Icelandic peninsula. Later, she visited it, noting in her talk 'Ecolinguistic Activism near Icelandic Glaciers', at the Flow and Fracture Symposium in Brussels, how 'what had been brown hair was now bleached nearly white . . . the hair was heavy with moisture . . . [and there had been] assimilation into the moss bed'. I had been fascinated by this fusion of moss and hair. It was so typical of moss to adopt, perhaps, to care.

In some Hindu ceremonies, the shaving of the head signifies rebirth, the removal of the old life and the start of the new. Our yogi has done this, in the past. The long locks she bears now have grown anew from a once-stripped scalp. Some make tonsuring pilgrimages, in accordance with an ancient myth concerning the god Vishnu. In this myth, Vishnu is hit on the head with an axe, losing a section of his hair. An angel offers a piece of her own to use in replacement and a grateful Vishnu accordingly grants wishes to anyone offering their hair in sacrifice. While in the Kenyan Masai tribe, men receive two ritualized head shaves to symbolize their initiation into different stages of manhood. The first comes after completing a training camp where boys learn to become warriors. The second marks the warrior's transition to an elder – a mature, married man, ready to move away from his father's home.

Am I ready to move away from my father's home? I have, but keep returning. Days ago, we had tended the grave. Mum had chopped away the grass, which had fallen haphazardly from her blade, leaving the mound shorn. I had scraped away the leaves and earth, wearing away the top layer of skin on a finger. I had touched the heads of the mosses as Mum had turned to leave. 'Have I left a bit?' she asked, concerned, but, seeing the mosses, smiled and said, 'Oh – you're talking to your friends.' On my father, or the living carpet over him, the haircut looked good. It had been clear, then, how cutting may be a form of tending, removing some shoots to allow for others. The same morning, Mum had cut the lilac bush. Each branch had been separated from its shoots, all the leaves had gone. In the afternoon, birds had come, lining the bare bark. For the first time in years, a hawfinch.

I had asked her, then, about her home – the one before this one, in Kenya – had she always lived there, as a child? Yes, she said. I asked for the stories of that place and its people. She had pushed down and pulled up a history. Old phrases and sayings came from deep recesses where they had lain, dormant, for decades. I asked her about the Masai: 'Yes, we were taught: "Keep away from the Masai, or they'll kill you with their spears." And another saying' – she had written it down, trying to remember – "*Mzungu aende ulaya, Mwafrika apate uhuru!*" – "White man go back to England, the African enjoy freedom".' She hadn't known what it meant, she said – as children, they had had to ask their parents. 'In fact, you asked, had I always lived there but I hadn't. We had lived, before, in another place but it was burned down in the night by the sick.' I wondered who she could mean. 'With their turbans and that British man with a whip.'

'Oh – the Sikhs?'

'Yes, the Sikhs, commanded by this man with the whip, rounding up those suspected of harbouring the Mau Mau – but they came for all the men, whether they were anything to do with the movement or not.' I heard the full story then, that had been buried for so long it had been forgotten. How the men were beaten and the houses burned and, on the other side, how the women – girls – were rounded up and taken to the bush to be the wives of Mau Mau soldiers. I heard how the uncle my mother had spoken of was, in fact, her father's uncle, a clan chief, exiled to England during the Emergency. And I took it all in. From the flames of the home she had lost, to the mirror her mother had hidden in the compost. It had been found and taken, like so much was found and taken, and, in the wreckage, the mirror had split.

'Yes, I still remember that whip.'

I let Warrior pose slip, moving my muscles from left to right, adjusting the pace, beginning to accelerate. As the head moves, the navel smooths a path from gut to speech, from which small words seep. In this Kundalini yoga, small mantras flit from the mouth as tension pours out. Then, in free movement, the body's orbit grows. No longer bound by the human, I dance as moss. First, the furry moss from the waterfall, that keyed out as *Thamnobryum alopecurum*, Fox-tail Feather-moss. Then, the mosses I know best: Kind Spears, Marilyn, Glowflake. I pull my body close to surfaces – walls, floors and alcoves. I go where a moss might go.

ICONIC

Thamnobryum alopecurum, Fox-tail Feather-moss

In a sack-back gown,
in Egyptian dress, as a saloon singer,
in a wrap-over dress: Vivien Leigh
in *Gone with the Wind*, Elizabeth Taylor
in *Cleopatra*, Marilyn Monroe in the *River
of No Return*, Kim Novak in *Vertigo*;
these women inhabit their green
as the limelight that tracks them, full-beam,
and as you, though you've never been
screened, hold the trees.

Mosses are thought to give more than they take, with the simplicity and small scale of their own needs, versus the many services they provide for others – building soil, purifying water, giving homes to invertebrates. Yet, they also know about self-preservation, how to streamline and to thrive on very little, how to whittle life down so that minimal effort is required from themselves, so that minimal effort is required to excel. This, I learn from the mosses – how to gather my needs in, to give without depleting – a warrior of retreating.

Lying, on the ground that will always be there, I breathe in and out – as hair that falls when no longer needed, the breath enjoys its new freedom. Waves fall in and swirl in small rockpools. Like starting a jigsaw, I lay out each part, each component of living, with a new sense of their relative importance, though I can't yet see how they might fit together. It will be months from now that a picture will emerge. Then, I will stare, dazed, at the new composition of my life, wondering how it came to look like that, but for now I only move the pieces around. As though waking from a dream that you try to reach your hand back into, to draw out the fleeting episodes, to try to connect them – that is the work I do now. In the few days spent out of the limelight with the women and the mosses, and the many increments of time leading up to and away from them, I let the body do its dreaming, I get out of its way.

8. BRILLIANT

WILLINGTON GRAVEL PITS

I let the body do its dreaming. I get out of its way. But, a warren praying for soft occupants, tension builds as it waits. I want to tell it that it will be fine, that I am always fine when I am with M. But there are so many places for fear to seep in, an inordinate number of crevices. Perhaps it won't be rabbits. Perhaps it will be weasels. Perhaps it will be ribs and teeth – an iron blade. Perhaps it will coarse and sting and never fade. Whatever waits for the body. Whatever is waiting to move in. Perhaps it will be the last thing I ever know, before thought leaves and all recedes but the fury of a scorching grief.

There are terrible fates for the body but I needn't imagine them all. I needn't go through every possible breakage in advance of its arrival. It takes a conscious jolt to remember this, like plugging myself in. And though I want to welcome lightness, to be easy with myself – as I have learned how to now, as I must not forget how – I still can't help but ask: will I be able to live up to this joy? This billowing meadow that grows at the very edge of myself – might it not give up on me? Might it not need softer pasture? I am still too much brink, too much precipice. Will we fledge, or fall? With all the boldness a body holds, I breathe deep and open my wings – my shoulder blades – as something sings.

A cuckoo. My first of the summer, the second for M. There are reed banks bordering the wetlands at the Willington Reserve in the Trent valley, and we think of the reed warblers' nests that are favourites for cuckoos to lay eggs in. The sound of the cuckoo transports me to two places at once: summer afternoons at the dining-room table in Devon, my father in an open-necked checked shirt, window open, the breathy call – Cuckoo, cuckoo. 'Hear it?' My father, all urgent enthusiasm. Simultaneously, my Devon grandparents' farm, wandering through the arable land, the spot above the cows by the brook where the bird would sound. It is like the Swahili double word for memory implies – two experiences by one portal sense tied. *Kumbukumbu*. Cuckoo, cuckoo.

As we get closer, the call is louder, more throttled and insistent. It is joined by the frantic caws of the gulls, which dominate now, the cuckoo infrequently punctuating. M hands me his binoculars but I have closed my eyes. With so much to hear, looking seems too much – a sensory overload. I open my eyes just as the cuckoo breaks cover and flies over our heads into trees on the other side. 'See how it looks like a bird of prey,' M says, guiding me through the paths he knows so well, his light shirt shimmering.

Every now and then I veer off-path, following moss, leaving M mid-sentence. After a while he gets used to the process, realizing my answer may come some time after he has spoken, I am on moss time now. In the hide, he has a more attentive audience as he talks to a birder friend about what's out there. Both become animated, as the conversation moves from birds to humans and the people they have in common. M sits back as the words ripple around him. His movements, smooth and languorous, can put others so quickly at their ease.

His friend talks of his retirement plan – 'I'm going to drive wherever I want in a day and then take a fortnight coming back.' I realize the protracted return will be filled with birding. It is an itinerant life, oddly in keeping with the birds he'll share it with. Each birder has a different story, a different reason for being here, and once more I don't know where to put my focus. On the birds, or on the mosses, or on the people?

As they speak again about what they've seen, I notice the language grow more possessive. 'Did you see the cuckoo?' 'I had it last week.' Why 'had' and not 'saw', or 'felt'? It's a very different hide experience than with Louise, when we mostly sit in silence. Here, there is constant talking, as the birders, all male, exchange what they've 'had'. When a woman with pink-and-blue hair enters they momentarily fall quiet – it changes the flow of the air inside, it adds a bold, new current.

I focus, finally, on the reed beds. The more I come to wetlands, the more the fringes attract. What is moving through the reeds? Whose bodies are resting? Who takes advantage of the flashy, higher birds, to remain hidden and undetected? I know they are there. Perhaps fear is, too, amid the mud, the marsh, the knotted grass. Perhaps it is cold and seeps all through this spot, garrottes each tiny neck and stops their little hearts. Or perhaps it is too soft here for it to even start. Fear likes a brittle pathway, all arch and shard and tension. The cushioned reeds, the grassy seeds do not offer easy access.

It can be tempting to cover over lightness. When you come upon a flash of brilliance, to try to keep it hidden from the dangers it might face. But there is no hiding from M. The edges between us have become so blurred, muddied, flooded over, that, as we walk back from the reserve, I realize there is no space left between us. Together, M and I have formed a new shape.

SHAPWICK HEATH

Lily pads drape over water, submerged leaves curling and frilling like Lollo Rossa lettuce as I look up. I reach a hide brimming with men in anoraks with large 'scopes. Their gaze turns from sky to path as I pass. Then, a woman glides by on a bicycle and we exchange smiles: two women in the wetlands, instantly smoothing the dent the gaze from the hide had made.

Camilla appears on the horizon, her outline glowing. She has caught the sun and, up close, I see her ruddy cheeks. She tells me she has been walking long distances around her Wiltshire home. I see the change the light has made in her, tanning and holding her in a warming blush. Our chatter flits and swerves with the fleeting bodies of insects in our path before turning to mosses. I say that something is emerging through my time with them, although much is still submerged. I think of my moss-swimming trajectory. From dangled fingers at Roudsea Woods, to leg-deep near Cors Fochno, then, further in, the whole body.

One of the few land plants to still produce swimming sperm, mosses have had to adapt since no longer surrounded by sea. While moss sperm use flagella, tiny threadlike structures, to help them swim, I have only legs, that, once in, are swiftly rooted. I have only arms, that get tangled in the rope-like rhizoids. Yet, with typically only an hour to live, the pressure is intensified on their watery quests. We walk by the high reeds and broken-down Sphagnum in the surrounding peat, thinking of this mossy bravery, the unwillingness to accept defeat. As we duck in and out of shade and into the dapple of willow we find mosses scattered over banks, pillowing the pathways. *Orthodontium lineare*, Cape Thread-moss, shoots a firework display where young green capsules drop off vivid seta, tiny firings of lime. Growing in patches, fields of gleaming embers, the wavy leaves bend away from the rest of their bodies. The capsules, dangling at an angle, seem tired of carrying so much light. I picture myself at Willington, how I had willed myself open to another, how I had made the nervy crossover. With all the courage a body holds, the mosses carry their glowing load. I wonder how many of their spores will fall, how many brave swims will strike out over leaf.

FIREWORK

Orthodontium lineare, Cape Thread-moss

There goes the rush of you – flushed through and blushed with a capsuled dew – there's just no stopping you. The faint-hearted far better not start it, you are in front before you've departed.

Still, you hang your head like a jewel. We all need fuel. You can't endlessly burst with all colours dispersed, without ever a pillow for the parts that hurt. Let me pick you up. Not from the ground but the middle. The part of the branch that is hidden. Will it help if I tell you, you're winning? You're so far out in front you're beginning a new race, a new layer of space – a firework with so much at stake. You hurtle through peat and stone and bark, the whole of you committed to swallowing dark. And the absence of night is not enough for your light, yours is the kind that must fight and fight but there is far more to you than what you're able to do for others.

When your body is sore, lay it down. When the air is an effort, touch ground. You can be tired. Rest. Be a lull – knowing fire can never be dull.

Over cider, we discuss what we have seen. The only women in the pub, it takes a while for our sheen to wear off, for us to drop from eye-line. I think of the firework moss – how *Orthodontium lineare* had seemed to want to lay its light down. How it looked tired of being on show, of others needing its performance, when, perhaps, all it wanted was to grow in its own way, without bother, to be brilliant but not smothered, to be dazzling but privately, an unchecked part of the scenery. The woman in the hide at Willington, and the one who cycled past here stay with me. As the mosses swim to new places, we too, strike out to landscapes where our faces may differ from the norm. The women in the wetlands don't always conform. They wear the weight of a gaze, guided by mosses who blaze regardless of any onlooking lens.

CHEVIOT HILLS AND FORSINARD FLOWS

I look again at the places the mosses have taken me; from raised bogs and Bronze Age cists on Devon moors to my present journeying, edging north, always pivoting on the Midlands, the country's navel. Largely by rail and on foot, along the margins of a working week, or at the term's end in a flurried movement streak, I have made my way. Not a grand expedition with thoughts of conquest but taking each opportunity that comes to meet the moss on its terms, gradually coming to learn some part of what it teaches.

At length, I reach the Border Mires. Along the Roman Wall up to the Scottish border at Kielderhead, these habitats form part of what was once the largest continuous tract of blanket bog across northern England. At the summit of the Cheviot, the highest peak in Northumberland National Park, a large peatland restoration project hopes to prevent around 585 tonnes of carbon dioxide from entering the atmosphere each year. The park has a female head ranger, Margaret, for the first time in its history. The area, with its elevation, is a tough one to explore – I ask Margaret to tell me more.

'We have been planting Sphagnum mosses up there with volunteers and staff, with help from the local farmers and keepers to transport the plants up onto the tops. These were normally done in two-day stints, the first day collecting the plants and the second day planting them.' As well as the Cheviot planting, she tells me about similar work with mosses at Greenlee Nature Reserve, along Hadrian's Wall.

I stand at the water's edge. Stretching out my arms, I make a crossroads of the body. Eastward, and further north, lies the ossuary of the Bamburgh bones. Along that coastline, bones from 1,400 years ago rose to the surface of the dunes in a storm. From their image, I shift once more into the forest at Borth, that, after rough weather, leaves the sea to stand tall, as though the water had ever ebbed, as though the forest had never left. To live in moss time is to be in many timeframes at once, to live in moss space is to access many places in one jump – I throw my bones up, leap high into blue, landing with a new draft of what I once knew.

I crouch down, looking out across the boardwalk. While draining for agriculture and afforestation has damaged these peatlands, there has been significant restoration in Northumberland's bogs, involving the damming of ditches and tree removal. I feel the mark of Margaret's work in this place, the careful stewarding trace. By blocking the ditches, the water table can rise, soaking the mosses as more water is stored in the peat. Lying down, at full stretch, I consider my body as part-dam. No longer a ditch to fall into but a soft edge that protects you. Re-wetting is an important part of restoration. I feel my bones come to the surface. I feel the bones of others work loose. I see the women rising from the Bamburgh dunes.

In the absence of their known names, archaeologists have given these risen bodies Old English codewords – words from the time they lived in but not their original names and not claiming to be. There is an acceptance of unknowing in this approach that makes naming easier to broach. I think of my earlier moss kennings of star-grass and leaf-glass – might an element of doubt be added? A prefix of unknowing that might lead us to say: *From my place of not knowing, I offer you star-grass. From my place of not knowing, I offer you leaf-glass.*

From their place of not knowing, archaeologists have examined soil extracts in the teeth, receiving clues as to where these people may have come from. Some are described, as can be seen in the Bamburgh Bones digital ossuary, as 'non-local but British', others from 'outside Britain, and far to the south'. While this information may in itself challenge some perceptions of belonging, moss time says this is too small a frame for an origin, moss space says we all go further back and deeper in. The body of one middle-aged Bamburgh woman has notches in her canines suggesting that she repeatedly held something in her teeth, perhaps in an action involved in basket-making. I am drawn to this woman weaver in the wetlands, as one who, too, stitches repeatedly through wet ground. I learn that her codeword is '*Untwēoġendlic*', meaning undoubtedly. Containing the word '*twēode*' – doubtful, a shadow of unknowing slips through. It feels like a helpful addition – the opposite of 'Amen', for what we don't know is true.

By the time I reach the Flows, I have felt the movement of many bones. The Bronze Age cremation from the Crock of Gold dispersed, the Anglo-Saxon Bamburgh women risen in a burst of sand, a forest standing in sea, bark-bones stretched ahead of me; so that when I reach the tract of Scottish bog, I am completely bone-logged. Run-through with the bodies of the past, floating backward and forward in the glittering task of aliveness.

The Flow Country across Caithness and Sutherland is home to the world's most intact and extensive blanket-bog system. In this kind of peatland, formed in high rainfall and cool temperatures, plants don't completely rot away when they die but accumulate to form vast stretches of peat – ten metres deep in parts. Looking out across Forsinard Flows, the largest RSPB nature reserve in the UK, I slow. Everything here is on a vaster scale than I have known.

Amid such largeness, I can feel too small to make a difference. But that is the magic of brilliance – each droplet is luminous.

Remembering the Willington reeds with their small seeds of intimacy, I curl up by the moss leaves. When the body is bold enough to soften, selves start to layer and cross in evolving tapestries. I rest on the Sphagnum, years deep, blanketed, falling asleep as the journey's mosses replay behind closed eyes: the slender stars of Common Haircap forming brittle constellations, *Hylocomium splendens* spreading glowing invitations, plaited *Hypnum* in the dappled pine beneath and *Sphagnum austinii* pressed in between the reeds – all a flashing brilliance in the dark folds of sleep.

BRILLIANT

Hylocomium splendens, Glittering Wood-moss

Besides being brilliant
most need the people who say they are brilliant
who buy them brilliant lunches
and hoover brilliant carpets
who hold up brilliant mirrors
and paint their brilliant varnish
who listen to them practise their brilliant little speeches
hiding all that isn't brilliant from their upper brilliant reaches
they need a brilliant silence which others must observe
a tower of brilliant cushions to soothe their brilliant nerves
a brilliant little party to show their brilliant face
a brilliant invitation for only brilliant guests
they need brilliant conversation to flex their brilliant brains
a rugged, brilliant freedom which cannot be contained,
yet, you who are only brilliant, with nobody to see
bear all the world's light in all your light worlds of quiet
electricity.

REDEEMER
Hypnum cupressiforme, Cypress-leaved Plait-moss

If I were good, you would be my bones
yours the ribs inside me sewn
so when I breathed it would be your chest
on which my breath would come to rest.
If I were good, you would be my tissue
threads of plaited, growing tinsel
rustling deep inside my arms
each time I moved, each time I tired.
So when I came at last to sleep
I would be wholly yours to keep
having so much good from you
as to be redeemed, in full.

WILD SLEEP
Sphagnum austinii, Austin's Bog-moss

Warm in the reeds, the small dragon breathes
in leaves – hummocks of air kick up their lair

of long living, ancient and hidden in the hoarding
peat – this is a gentle heat that lends its colour

to the bog, an orange and ochreous fog that glowing
rises, its open mouth lets the skies in, through wild sleep.

COEDYDD MAENTWROG,
A WELSH RAINFOREST

As the darkness retreats, we greet the summer dawn. We are try-ing to make the most of the last days of warmth, though, this time, when Louise suggested a rainforest, I was not so easily taken in. The last one we had visited at Coed Felinrhyd had been warm and soggy and dripping with mosses, but, in terms of size and loca-tion, not quite what one might expect from a rainforest. Yet, its humid climate and habitat untouched by grazing or deforestation has allowed sessile oak and hazel to grow undisturbed since the ice age giving it as much right to the name as any more exoticized location.

The Atlantic oak woodland at Coedydd Maentwrog, our objective this time, is a unique habitat where the mosses that need a humid climate to grow in can thrive. The spray from the streams, together with the high rainfall and shade from the trees, keeps the air humid, allowing the moisture-loving mosses to grow along the oak tree-trunks, rocks and across the forest floor. These oak woods are a fragment of the wide Atlantic wildwood that once stretched down the west of Britain and Ireland, now creating rare temper-ate rainforest. Although we scramble down steep paths and over rocky river gorges, with swathes of serpent moss-green all around, we are not quite as intrepid as Amazonian explorers. In fact, fresh from tea and cake at the Tan y Bwlch Station Café, where a work-ing steam train chugs by at regular intervals, we can still make out the bright billow of bunting and the glint of china in the sunlight. Nevertheless, there is a boldness to our small-scale travel and we soon make our own discoveries.

The neighbouring Ceunant Llennyrch woodland is home to the rare *Sematophyllum demissum*, Prostrate Signal-moss, the unusual *Campylopus setifolius*, Silky Swan-neck Moss and *Leptoscyphus cuneifolius*, Wedge Flapwort. But in the woodland we pass through, we see the more common *Dicranum scoparium*, Broom Fork-moss and *Plagiothecium undulatum*, Waved Silk-moss. It is not the rarity of these mosses that holds our interest, nor, particularly, the ability to identify them, but rather, the freshening feeling of being in their company, the chance to make new acquaintances and to greet old friends. *Plagiothecium undulatum* gives a warming echo of a moss found when keying out the Cinder Path in Devon – *Plagiothecium denticulatum*, Dentated Silk-moss – now known to me as Gentle Fire.

Of all the mossy inhabitants we pass, it is *Dicranum scoparium*, Broom Fork-moss, that is the most clearly fertile. Long yellow-and-red setae bear orange capsules in a fiery gathering of waiting spores. This moss is sometimes known as 'Windswept Broom' because of the messy sweep of its leaves, but wind also plays a part in its repro-duction. When the long-beaked, membranous hoods, or *calyptrae*, which cover the capsules, fall to the ground, a ring of sixteen teeth is revealed. The spores in each capsule are released to the wind through the circular opening between the teeth. It is extraordinary to think of these tiny teeth opening amid the boom of our footfall. I open my mouth and puff, a little human steam train, through the hot moss-toothed terrain, as curious as any Amazonian explorer, with just as much to gain.

PLUNGE

Plagiothecium undulatum, Waved Silk-moss

A thousand embraces in a clutch of soil
a hundred heartaches catching in the roil
of rushing leaves, body against body in
the heave of connection. We may change
direction but risk a position worse than this,
a rift, with no part of me touching no part of
you, with no part of me touching nobody
new, with no easy way out of the wave
now we're in, shall we swim?

STRIKE

Dicranum scoparium, Broom Fork-moss

What would you sweep away if you could
dredging the gold from the gorse
wedging the sun between stalks
smothered in heather
      because you lit the fire but nobody came
you pick the edge of the heath until it frays
in the fringes scour for the light
you couldn't save.

CORS CARON

Louise and I feel our spirits drain on what we realize will be our last bog visit for a while. We are bold explorers now – bog dancers – and want to go on and on in the bogscapes, not in buildings, not in seminar rooms or offices. Yet, the oppressiveness of incoming schedules is soon countered by the wide expanse of the bog. Cors Caron is a nature reserve of vast wetland filling the valley of the River Teifi, near Tregaron, that includes three raised bogs – peat that has accumulated over 12,000 years. For us, the landscape is a true restorative.

We are reminded, though, of the work still to be done to elevate bogs from the wastelands they used to signify in the cultural imagination by a visitor board at the site. 'At one time many people saw Cors Caron as a wilderness standing in the way of progress,' the board states, outlining the area's rail history. I think of all the bogs marked 'wildernesses' on maps, the interchangeability of these words in the past. On the signage, the ingenuity of the nineteenth-century engineer, David Davies, is celebrated, for lowering bales of wool and twigs into wet bog, underpinning the railway line for a service that ran until 1965. In Davies' time, Cors Caron was referred to as 'the red bog on the banks of the Teifi'.

All day, the colour haunts us. First, there is a soaring red kite who we follow out across the terrain. We are the visitors here and it is the guide, though it may have no thought of us following. Then, we find the people on the boardwalk are dressed, every one, in red. From head to foot, sock to hat and lower, still, than that, to the bloom of the sundew in the mosses and the deep blush of *Sphagnum magellanicum* (the favourite moss of Margaret, head ranger at Northumberland Park), to the water in the bog itself, reddened by humic acid and the rosy reflection of it all.

The *Sphagnum magellanicum* – which has been recently reclassified with a change of name to the less sonorous *Sphagnum medium* – reproduces asexually here. Bent down low, I follow the glint of the branch leaves, the light tips of the capitula, to where, beneath, deeper plum bodies grow their robustness of red. It is humbling to think of these bodies reproducing themselves in the ground without any of the technology required to make Dolly the sheep, or Barbara Streisand's cloned dogs.

MARS

Sphagnum magellanicum, Magellanic Bog-moss

In the core of the web, in the warp
and weft of a world made red you are
centreless, your stain is relentless – hold
my skin, as I just step off the planet,
there are lights here that know no damage
there is scent here without its trapping,
a universe unwrapping.

To think about what is in the human body that is irreducible and unreproducible is to pull from the peat ancient words like spirit, like soul. So saturated are they now, after years of accretion, that they are hard to handle – slippery relics from which it can be difficult to find new meaning. The Modern English word 'soul' is thought to derive from the Old English '*sáwol*', or '*sáwel*', with one early instance coming in the poem *Beowulf*. While the poem's date of composition is not known, some believe it to be around the eighth century, and that the manuscript that remains today was copied by scribes in the early eleventh century. *So it is poetry that keeps a hold of these things*, I think, as we reach a spot where a sundial rises from the reeds. It is easy to see what has been unearthed when the light shines fully dispersed. I think of my mother, who, as the sun had dripped in, had seen a home she had hidden. How the memory had surfaced in slithers, of an earlier home burned to cinders. It is a picture that I now inherit, as the meaning of home glows, transparent.

'Poetry', says Audre Lorde in 'Poetry Is Not a Luxury' from *Sister Outsider*, 'forms the quality of light within which we predicate our homes and dreams toward survival and change'.[11] If our homes have been burned and moved on, if our homes have been buried and blown, there is bold work of the spirit to do, in the conjuring of something new. That, my grandmother knew, reshaping lost land in Embu.

A Gitukia song of that place, 'The Whiteman is by Thagana River' ('*Mucungu Ari Runjiiri*'), recorded and translated by H. S. K. Mwaniki in *Categories and Substance of Embu Traditional Songs and Dances*,[12] is danced before the millet harvest. It recalls the threat approaching the border of the last Kikuyu stronghold. The singer suggests that a cord be thrown over to the enemy to help him cross the river, safe in the knowledge that it will break and he will drown. The song contains the phrase '*Ui ui*', a lament that the translator finds no equivalent for in English; '*Ui ui angirega gukua niagutuika na muugu*' – 'Ui ui, if he doesn't die, the cattle-hide cord will break and he will fall [into the river]'.

In *Beowulf*, the threat has already crossed over the wetland, as Grendel leaves his fen lair to do battle in the very hall of the warriors. Yet, he retreats, defeated, back 'under the fen-banks' – 'under fenhleoðu' (l. 820), and, at his death, the fen water turns red as 'there the water was surging with blood' – '*Ðær wæs on blōde brim weallande*' (l. 847).[13]

As I stand on the red bog on the banks of the Teifi, I think of how these bloodshot waters run through me – how I sing of battle, threatened homes and waters but as their daughter – a warrior of softening, a poetry of slipperiness. When I pull a word from the bog it is '*ui*' – the repeated cry of Kikuyu lament. When I pull a word from the bog it is '*wea*' – the Old English for woe; '*wealafe*' is a woeful remnant. Once, in *Beowulf*, this woe appears as: '*wēan onwendan*' (l. 191)[14] – woe that never stops. Perhaps we are all '*wealafe*' – living remnants of woe. We are the '*alead*' – the living and the dead. We dip our skin in a liquid history. We see through to the bottom of the sea. Red waters are mosses that pull up embossed with a sweetening survival, a song of revival.

On this equinoctial day, the light drops over the dial like a shawl, which is needed now the nights are drawing in and winter approaching. But this light is not just any item of clothing. It is forged in the sun and from the months spun and it waits, like all dates, for no one. We eke out the last few hours from the day and from the summer, bathed in a brilliant sheen, in the low-down sway of the reeds and the lower-still glosses of peat, our heads buried deeply in mosses. When we remember to look up, the sky bursts like a fresh volcano as a kite blasts red wings against wide blue. Following, as it lifts, soars, arches, I focus on how to mould the light.

9. LITTLE PEACH

BIRMINGHAM

In the darkness, mosses show us how to hold the light. The lilt along leaf, branch, spore – lifts, soars. From the beginning of midwinter's night to its end, I hear it, washing against the back door. I step out into the small space I do not own and listen to it grow. As the wind threads between the bodies, a music builds. These rootless plants begin to fill with a song of grounding where they're blown, with ways of making a not-home, home. I feel their song inside me. Does my body house a room to be filled, or a buried love, that longs to be tilled? When my father left, I learned about emptiness but this – this feeling that there is something new, waiting to be summoned – is fresh, is dew. What song does a mother who is not a mother sing? What is she awakening?

Mosses' rootless, small-leaved bodies don't make flowers to entice pollinators or to shroud the intricacies of reproduction. Instead, sporophytes catch the eye like flashing glow-sticks. Some may be muted in colour and less outwardly striking, yet, when you do notice them, you find they hold their own power to mesmerize: thin bodies tapering, the dangled threads of a delicate tapestry. Spores released from mature capsules grow into new plants, or parts of a stem or leaf may break off to regenerate. Flowerless, but with multiple reproductive processes, mosses show there is more than one way to mother.

Not the flashiest bodies in the earth, they can refrain from the more popular trappings of beauty and don't have to spend days saying: *Look at me*. Yet, they are not completely alone. There may not be a male and a female partner – in some cases, there is no partner at all. But even without a partner, they need the right conditions for growth. They need the dew and the rain to gather and clothe.

The wash of the mosses outside stirs the turn of the words

inside, as memory sifts an old poem I once learned: 'I Syng of a Mayden', that has been put to music and is still sung today. In this Middle English lyric, included in Douglas Gray's *English Medieval Religious Lyrics*, the arrival of Jesus is compared to the dew: 'He cam also stylle ther his moder was / As dew in Aprylle that fallyt on the gras' (ll. 3–4).[15] Mary is aligned variously with grass, flower and spray, and, yet, it is moss that flourishes though it bears no flower, as Mary gave birth without the giving of hers.

Now, not in the April of this poem but the deep dark of December, I think, too, of the *Advent Lyrics*. A copy lies between the covers of the Exeter Book, housed in Exeter Cathedral, perhaps since 1050, when Bishop Leofric moved the episcopal see from Crediton to Exeter. I picture their journey, from my home town to home city, wondering if they found peace in their new surroundings. I should like to ask them – to go there now, in the depth of the dark strike out over 200 miles, take the book in my hands and enquire of the words that live there whether they have found rest between the laminated covers, under a vaulted ceiling of a building made for an invisible god.

In the second of these Advent poems, also included in Jackson J. Campbell's *Advent Lyrics of the Exeter Book*, Mary is described as a mother – a feat 'accomplished without the love of a man' (l. 20). The materiality of plants is prominent in the symbolism where 'All spiritual gifts sprang up throughout the earth; / then many a shoot became illumined' (ll. 24–5).[16] Elsewhere, Mary's body is compared to a garden. I wonder about my own. I suspect it is a bog: a vast surface of Sphagnum, glinting into the distance. A space that seems empty but isn't. A space that stretches down, holding histories, keeping the dead and the dying but also the living cellulose.

I step further into the house, leaving the door open, not letting go of the mosses but wanting to hear the human added. Different recordings ring out, yet, there is something missing, some connection I am unable to reach. Then, the sound of the maydens drifts in: the slow surge of voice over low organ's throat, the lapping of lungs, lilting onto shore. The first cathedral to allow girls to sing was Salisbury Cathedral, in 1991 – such a recent admission of such a large body of voices. It is the Ely Cathedral Girls' Choir that now joins the motion of the mosses. Their re-claiming of a song that once sang *of* a mayden now sung *by* maydens, prompts a charge along the blood that was absent before. As their voices repeat: 'He cam also stylle ther his moder was / As dew in Aprylle that fallyt on the gras', the mosses slip in through the open door. As the voices wash across the floor, the sound of both bodies meeting rings pure. My own begins to shift and lift in greeting.

As I continue to listen, another song starts to take hold. 'There Is a Flower' is a song I remember singing as a child. Its words are attributed to the fifteenth-century English poet and priest, John Audelay. The haunting opening by a female soloist with the Cambridge Singers affects the blood, just as before. It is as if my cells are tipped with wicks that are lit; a flickering light along the veins. And as the rich, incoming voices thicken the sound, it is as though the mosses have risen from the leaf-lit ground and my body is a halo around all this movement, all this music.

I hope others can hear it. Yet, I know that many don't. I wonder if field recordings of mosses singing of mosses could stir human listeners the way maidens singing of maydens can, but suspect that such wholly mossy music would still remain hidden to some. Perhaps, then, the earlier work to be done, in letting others into a moss-driven song, might be in translation – in human voices singing, however incompletely, of mosses. As I listen to Audelay's words, included in E. K. Chambers and F. Sidgwick's *Early English Lyrics*, that draw again on Marian symbolism, I hear the gaps that the mosses, if they were only noticed, could fill. 'There is a floure sprung of a tree, / The rote thereof is called Jesse, / A floure of price, / There is none seche in Paradise!' (ll. 1–4).[17] I start inserting mosses.

There is a *moss* sprung of a *spore*. The root*less shore of forest floor* / A *moss* of price, / A *pearl of plants* in Paradise. It is an act of re-claiming – shining light on the mosses who, while themselves so often overlooked, have brought so much brightness to me. These plants belong in our literature, in our small songs and spells, in our incantations of living and what it is to dwell. And amid all this light lie the descriptions we give mothers – as radiant, as glowing. It is how I speak of the flowerless mosses. Firework – 'blushed with a capsuled dew'; Gentle Fire's 'Stem of suns' that are 'sugar-spun' and *Sphagnum palustre*, with its flush of peach. In the tiny suns who fertilize without flowers there is so much endeavour, such hidden power.

LITTLE PEACH

Sphagnum palustre, Blunt-leaved Bog-moss

Baby's breath, lamb's bleat, little peach. Sleek of pulp and feet.
Cream. Loud pealing of bells. Dream. Pillows of plants, gleam the
grass together. Stitch. Branches tether leaves, no sleeves, a narrow.
Taper. Candles breaking in the grass. Shrink of throat and heart
won't pass. Your ditch-ripe cheeks, your pastel heat. Palustre is
a marsh but if you're classed by where you come from you're
the edge that meets the soften, you're the coughing of blossom
giving way to wood. Woven leaves, no sleeves, a shallow. Pink is
an afterthought. Peach is the leaf you brought. Your fleshy soft
and outer. Your hard a nutless butter. Nothing in that isn't soft.
Nothing out that isn't soft. Nothing in that isn't soft. Nothing
out that isn't soft. Stitch a sunset using ditches. Stitch a life using
peaches. See it grow. In the marshes no one knows what patterns.
Peek. Little quilt of heat. Fingertips dust sleep. Palustre, palustre,
creeps along the marrow, weaving pinks of mallow in the flushes,
butter-blushes.

Mosses, used in some cultures to line nappies and growing on my father's grave, are present at the start, as well as the end, of human lives. Now that my father's earthen plot is bathed in Sea Wrinkle (*Rhytidiadelphus squarrosus*), I feel more materially the potential of these plants to give solace, and how, with their soft coverings, they are, in truth, our final care-givers. While a doula supports a woman through birth, Sea Wrinkle, the graveside moss, is a kind of death doula – softening the impact of the departed.

In Kenya, Grandmother Isabella had been a traditional birth assistant in her village, helping mothers who could, or chose, not to go to hospital. Often too far to reach, or expensive to afford, there were also those who did not trust the doctors, as well as a stigma around the impersonal treatment received from them. I cannot tell if mosses found their way into these deliveries, though their adoption in bandages is well-known. Sphagnum mosses were used to dress wounds during wartime and mosses have been used by women as absorbent sanitary products during menstruation. There is nothing that mosses haven't seen, there is nowhere that they haven't been. There at our most fertile moments and when we have ceased to be – mosses know the shapes of our bodies, how they are mutable and house different needs.

In the Advent poem, the ground is not a site of loss but a more generative space where plants are 'illumined'. The earth's ability to grow plants is a wonder both compared to and dwarfed by that of Mary's immaculate conception. Mosses, the miraculous plants who generate new life without flowers, fit dazzlingly into the cultural symbolism of motherhood and plants. Yet, theirs is not a trope often, or even at all, explored. Perhaps it took a mother who is not a mother, to see it.

A mother who is not a mother – yet is. A birther of words, who senses that something is coming but without knowing its shape nor any time or certainty of arrival. A not-mother, who is lit, like the mosses, from rhizoid to tip and set adrift in water and bound by its rhythms and flushed through like a prism. A not-mother, an is-mother, a lit-mother, a fit mother. Perhaps there are many mothers like this, whose stories have been eclipsed. We can hear them all if we choose it – we can make our own music.

DERBYSHIRE

We make our way through strips of turf around M's mother's house, covered in Sea Wrinkle – a reassuring echo of my father and a way, this Christmas, of having him with me. Derbyshire is drizzling, with sun in small patches between rain – perfect for the mosses. I want to bend down and touch them but am aware of human eyes around the cul-de-sac. I settle for nudging M and pointing.

'Moss,' he asserts.

'Moss,' I agree. On Christmas morning, the garden is lit with blue-tits. Over the neighbouring houses, in the distance, high factory towers claim sky and eye. Then, something flits into foreground. 'Look,' I say.

'Sparrowhawk!' The word goes off in my head and out of M's mouth. It is an unlikely visitor to the suburban garden, a flash of wild that comes to me, reminding me of home.

M was introduced to birding by his father, who passed away around the same time as mine. There is a sense of legacy in this continuity of pastimes between the generations. I feel it when I am in the fields I shared with my father, when I celebrate those that grew with us there; the lives in and on the soil and in the air. Now, M retreats to tell his mother and I hear him join her at an upstairs window, looking out. I think of all the times my mother and I have done this – the countless mornings trading bird findings, passing our tiny wormy nuggets between us. Sparrowhawks are not unusual visitors to our Devon garden but still more frequent are kestrels and, our favourite, *Shamba Rafiki* – garden friend, a tawny owl. Although I am in a new place, these more-than-human neighbours ground me.

'I've written a carol about moss,' I announce, as we walk by the small places M has known since childhood – the lane that leads to the park, the roof of the building he used to climb.

'Let's hear it,' he replies. When faced with the direct task of singing about flowerless mosses and the Virgin Mary, I buckle.

'It's . . . still in development,' I mutter. But as we pass a church, I can't help but confess, 'I'd like to hear children sing it – a choir, maybe.'

'That's a lovely idea,' M says, valiantly, while knowing little of what I'm talking about. I wonder if it will happen. Bringing others in to the thing that only you have seen can be risky. But I have learned a little more about how to work together from the mosses and a little about hope, too – that there is no use saying no to the thing before it even begins. I think of my bog body, my moss quarry, my halo, my leaf-glow, my peach hue, my glimpsed dew and how I do not yet know what is coming through but that I want to let it, that I must accept it.

BIRMINGHAM

I try to feel connected on this day marking the date the international Convention on Wetlands was agreed at the Ramsar Convention in Iran, honouring a pledge for national action and international cooperation to conserve wetland habitats. But, as I flick through images from across the world from my urban home: coral reefs and mangroves shielding coastlines, Scottish peat bogs, stretches of Sphagnum I have come to cherish in Wales, it is easy to feel displaced. I think of what my own role is; a writer who draws attention to the mosses' gifts, who reports how restoring peatlands could be an act that lifts, who tries through acts of mossy friendship, however small, to build a sense of family that might keep an open door.

And it is good, when things feel too big, to start with something little. To find the moss closest to you and consider if you might begin to feel different in its presence – to catch something of its iridescence. I stare into the folds of the Bud (*Sphagnum capillifolium*) resting on my desk. The need to be near water is strong but it reminds me to start small, that bodies of water needn't be sprawled.

M and I make our way to the local brook. Today, it is me showing him the way; there are few places now that we haven't shared. Shoulders lower and ribcage rises as I catch its first glint. The trees on either side form no forest, the scrubland no meadow and the drizzled water over stone no bog or coral reef, yet, there is life here and my body adjusts to it, feeling a pleasure in its presence.

'I start to feel outside the city here,' I say to M, who nods and signals.

'Song thrush!'

A little further in, he points to the limelight on the floor. He's noticing the mosses now, just as Louise does and my mother, too. I feel a little glow at my attention becoming theirs, at the mosses moving into their lens. Dropping to the ground to tease apart the leaves, I reach identification. '*Kindbergia praelonga*,' I announce. 'Kind Spears,' I say more softly, to no one in particular. I notice a carpet of it off to the left and make my way there as M stands midway between the call of two thrushes. 'Scarlet elf-cups!' I motion him over.

'Do they grow as part of the mosses or are they separate?' he asks. I feel his question with my gut. Is this green space part of the city, or is it separate? A knot in the belly. Am I part of you now, or am I separate? The knot grows steadily.

'Separate,' I say but am never more conscious of a word not conveying its meaning, of saying something that is right but isn't true. The Oneida Nation people have placed scarlet elf-cups on the navels of newborns to promote healing. Once more, the maternal qualities of the flowerless suggest themselves, ring through. And I think again of the bonds that come from the centre of the body, making the boundaries of our bodies bend, turning us, some-how, into friends. In this little nook of fungi and mosses, with the thrushes stringing bars over and through us, with their notes scat-tered in between, we become part of the pattern. The drip of the water over stone and the pulse of the moss by the bone of my ear, an open cup, and the flash of the scarlet and the rush of the strings between us; tightening, not gripping; lightening, nothing slipping; hold us in a connective tissue.

Back at the house, M prepares to return to Derbyshire and I for another landlocked week. I wonder how long the brook's contact will last, when I will next need to recharge. Yet, looking at the Sphag-num on the table as it waits to spring back to life at the first new drop of water, not caring how long the wait has been, not defeated or dwelling on what has been, I sense a better way of responding to dry seasons. My body as a wetland of mostly water has ways to store there all the succour it needs. It is a kind of belief. Like a seed. Like a pearl. Like a net. Like yeast. Like all the hidden treasure in a field.

THE CINDER PATH

It was a long endeavour that revealed, early last year, the mosses along the Cinder Path. This time, with my young niece, it is the work of an instant.

'You can show me the flowers you know and I'll show you the mosses.' We strike a deal that is instantly forgotten in the rush of running free and fast downhill.

'What flowers have you seen?' I ask.

'I have no idea,' comes the speeding reply. Eventually, 'Snow-drops! Daffodils! Crocus!' as she lands with a thud in the grass by my feet.

'Do you know what moss is?' She looks sheepish.

'Well, I do . . . but I've forgotten.' I show her a gleaming gath-ering of Kind Spears and Marilyn.

'What do you think, do you like it?' She nods, eyes glinting. 'Which do you prefer, this furry one, or this feathery one?' The reply is instant.

'The feathery one!'

'Common Feather-moss!' I explain. She holds it for a moment, small fingers pressed over smaller leaves. Then, it is on with the breathless charge of forward motion.

'Come ON, Auntie!' Perhaps mossing is best left to those whose bodies have begun to appreciate slowness. She runs up and down the path, hair flying, wellington boots shining, stopping only to urge, 'What now? What NOW?'

When you have something growing inside you that is an absence but not an emptiness, how does one explain to others what it is that you are carrying? That it might be writing, or praising, or stewarding, or all of these things – the start of a joy that softly sings. It is simply the promise of something, although nothing visible is there. And you are holding a space and in that space is an idea of what may one day form. I think of the singing-back practices of the Warlpiri elders in the Tanami Desert and their efforts, reported by Barry Lopez in *Horizon*, to restore the mala wallaby. How they believe that, in a spiritual sense, the animals are still present, despite being declared locally extinct by scientists, and how a ritual process of singing might encourage the physical form of the animals to manifest once more.

The mosses on this path grow out of the cinder, new life rising from what has once been burned. Sometimes it is the space you hold that matters most. Sadness may teach you that when a hearth has opened inside and something enters and catches alight, that you must be alert to that first outward ember. You must be on standby with enough water to dampen it back down before it becomes generally known. Far better for there to be no trace of it (sadness will say, gripping its bucket) than to have any reminder, should it not, then, go on to live. Far better not to want anything at all (sadness whispers, each time you come to look at that ember, each time you are drawn back in), so that when it doesn't come (it mouths triumphantly, like it is reaching its crescendo), you won't even have missed it.

But when you listen, and start to unpick it, you find that sadness doesn't make sense at all. Music, with its deep bodily resonances, cuts through its chatter. And the mosses with their miniature choirs, make music from the very spires of their bodies, the high sporophytes that ignite with the wonder of flowerless light. There is little that sadness can say amid the sway of the stalks and shimmering talk of the mosses, in the shake of the spores as they, glimmering, fall. There are so many forms for happiness to take – I intend to find them all.

10. DAWN

DARTMOOR

There are so many ways for happiness to break and they all come
in a storm. The rain blazes and the mosses burn in a radiance past
glowing. There is a knowing in the way they give themselves over
to the flood – how the flash of the dark, beating, is a part of them –
how they lean into it, without turning away. With their deep bodily
resonances, the mosses capture the movement as music that runs
through them. Miniature choirs, they make music from the very
spires of their bodies. But I do not need to enter the rain to feel its
undoing. To know how its force will tear through me like a dog
and I will limp away without looking. The human shell of me. The
mess that skin can make of water, in its halfway house between
absorption and protection.

Though we cannot, like the mosses, be fully exposed to the elements, still – I think – we are miraculous. Rain moves off us like
wax. In the fold of the dark, we mutter and part our lips with the
drip of the cold pouring in. Still, we persist. If you strike a match
in the sky above us, we will not burn. We will not ignite in the dark
with leaf-light, but muffle with brick, the lick of it. We say things
to each other like *sigh*. Like saliva. Like the slow crackle of breath.
Safe in our houses, the small, domestic sounds of us go unrecorded.
Yet, we have a way of leaning, too, into difficulty. Not all at once,
with the openness of mosses in rain but with little shuffles of trust
that gain traction. Little shakes of the head, stretches of skin. Small
ways of saying, *Come in*.

I have been trying to lean into loss and to sound it, not with big
actions or loudness but the small notes that seep in with the morning. I want to find those words and slip them into a pool where
they might live submerged, ready to rise again like salmon, breaking the surface when needed – when joy has once more slipped

and sadness tightened its grip. That is when the words that speak of this without pounding – the words that voice this loss without drowning – are so necessary. Some of them, I am sure, must come from these early sounds – the little shuffles of the body waking. I think this, as I watch the wintry turn from night to morning, learning its daily lesson in survival. Not profound, not new but staggering in its repetition. From darkness, to the first smudge of something lighter. To the outlines. Horizon. Hills. One bird trills. The one that has the courage to make the first sound in deep dark. To the turn of a trill to a trickle. From a trickle to a choir. Daylight. Sun begins to colour in.

Flowers come. Floating lights in the branches. The impossibility of blossom in the dead of night. The incongruity of petals in the dark. And, yet, the way we greet each other afterwards, as though this deep miracle has not just occurred. 'Morning,' we acknowledge. But it means hello, not *look*. Not, *stop* – something outstanding has happened. I thought the world was dead but it was only a kind of blindness. I thought that I was dead but it was only kindness that had retreated and needed coaxing out. In the early hours, before the light, sadness can seem very loud. It will tell you there is nothing on the other side of it. It will tell you silence is the seam along which you will slip.

But silence is a kind of blood that works from the ground, up. Internal, integral; with tactile qualities – spaces that you can sit in and listen and wait, places to absorb, to draw in, inflate. For before the first words, there are the first rhythms. The deep rustle of sleep. The furl and unfurling of fingers. The touch of an eyelash. Perhaps, in this little language of waking there is a way in, bridging the ease of sleep with the alertness of awake – not counting as much as a full statement, nor taking as much from us.

Mosses hold a special kind of silence. They soak up light and seem to give out peace. In the branches, in the boughs, in the prows of the trees, they send and receive in the silent seas of the woods. Where sky and land shift and meet in the mosses, clouds of leaf, suns of leaves bring softness and kindness together in springing stillness. From here, they take me not to speech but music. I think of melodies as not only notes but pauses and of the empty bars that are equally a part of things and the times when notes sound together and the times when they don't and when one may sound alone – solo voices and choral tapestries. I hear us taking turns, to speak and to listen, to learn and to act and a shared music between humans and other species. I sense birds showing us where to begin, insects mesmerizing as we lean in, and beneath this, the absorbing fusion of silence and sound – the moss music murmuring just above ground.

I breathe in the gathering light and the trill of the thrush and the wash of the moss. I breathe out the end of the night and the thrill of the touch of new air and its gloss. And this coming and going is like the sound of the sea, from the back of the throat, a release. The deep crash of waves. A very small sound but one that is bathed in the strongest of elements, this first breath washes fresh over the night's sediments.

DAWN

Sphagnum subnitens, Lustrous Bog-moss

Powder pink, tiny blink, in amid the peaty sheets – first to wake in sunlight's tremble, full of stretch and sleepy shingle – all the detritus of dream, from your creamy leaflids gleams. Up, and up, and up you rise, high as ground and low as sky – yours are clouds that puff the peat, twirling like a tutu's pleats, pirouetting through the fog – Ballet Dancer of the Bog. How you came to be so nimble, lime-limbs wrapped in rosy dimples, is a mystery to us, unable to come close enough to the whirling of the planet, yet, through you we almost manage to be captured in the turns of the deep dance of the earth.

As I pull nearer to the Cave Valley mosses, I begin to hear the women who have brought me here. I hear the rustle – brushing past the acrocarps by Grandmother Lucy's old house – and the static, zooming in on digital Sphagnum near Grandmother Isabella's home. I hear Alys and Deb's guidance as the woodland widens, and Louise and Camilla, willing and eager. I hear Margaret with her stewarding attention and Trish's *living memory passed down by many generations*.

And Audre Lorde, too, is an undercurrent. From the dark of the storm in the night, to the start of the bird and the light, I have been hearing her thoughts on silence. In 'The Transformation of Silence into Language and Action', she said: '*We examined the words to fit a world in which we all believe*,'[18] as she weaved women's sounds with her own bright thread until sentences like constellations spread. And it feels this way with the women in the wetlands, with the women *and* the wetlands. When I move from a place of silence into a world in which we might believe and of the words that might fit them, it is one made of their voices, populated by mosses. Small collectives of voice that sing of a larger choice: to live in communities of care, where the overlooked might be looked after and share, in their turn, invitations to learn.

CAVE VALLEY

At the base of the fern, citrus mosses trill. Lemons and limes, gleaming. I cannot fathom how some do not see them. Yet, despite the vastness of their habitat and quality of light, they often go unnoticed except when their appearance marks them out as a target to be removed – weeds cluttering a manicured lawn. Bent down towards the primrose mosses, I pause. Have you ever spoken to a moss? Not with your mouth. Have you ever spoken to a moss with your silence? With that special porousness that is a spoken fluidness? That is what pulses from moss to moss and from the pit of the stomach to the grit of the clam, from one inside to another? With the silence that is listening and filling, holding and releasing? Have you ever silenced to, not spoken to? I wonder what my silencing to a moss looks like. Is it visible? Or simply another absence that, somehow, still manages to be in the wrong place.

I tread softly from moss mound to mound, finding the same plants whose heat I had touched a year ago, whose warmth had lit me as I let grief go. Now, I am not touching but listening. Bending my ear right down and waiting. My human ears, un-tuned to moss, cannot hear anything at first. It takes time to cleanse the palette of the air from human concerns, to filter through to moss. After several minutes, crouched awkwardly in the cold, I begin to hear the air make its way through the plants. The longer I stay, the louder it becomes. In time, it feels astonishing that I hadn't heard it before.

As I listen to the mosses, each group of gathered plants seems to offer a different part of the tune. The mosses on the trees and cave walls produce a high note, the mosses on the boulders, on the ground – a low reply. I begin to lend my voice to theirs. A high 'Ah' from the treetops, a low 'Oh' from the floor. In the mouth of the cave, white bones form a stave. I write down each sound: 'Ah-oh-oh-o-o-o-oh-a-a-ah', paying close attention as words take the place of incremental sounds. 'Ah' becomes 'I'. 'Oh' becomes 'know'. A long sequence of 'oh's form 'sorrow'. These sounds, together with the whip of the wind and the sting of the ice which begins to fall as hail, feel something like a singing sorrow.

From the high branches of the beech, I sing, as the hail falls in. 'Ah, oh – I know!' Sweeping down the ridge, 'Ohh, o o-o-ohhhhhh – your so-o-o-rrow.' Tripping among the boulders, 'La, la – la-aah, la, la – la-aa-aah – in the hai-l, in the hai-ai-il!' The enclosure fills with reverberating trills in a song that is open to anyone. The wind plays its part through the mosses whose dance directs its course as the hail bursts forth and the clatter of bark and the heave of the dark and the beating of wings and the pouring of things that have been dormant starts:

> I know your sorrow, in the hail, in the hail.
> Heart-torn and hollow, in the hail, in the hail.
> Moss will hold you like a glove,
> light you, lead you back with love.

For once, I feel my part in this is not harmful. By singing with the mosses, by joining in, I feel part of a microscopic kindness, a giving back on the tiniest of scales.

And the sun, when it comes, is caught by the primroses and the cluster of mosses around them. These, some of the first I had tried to identify myself, before any short-cuts provided by small banks of stored knowledge made the process easier, had tested my ability to stay with what I didn't know, to try to relate to the inscrutable. *Isothecium alopecuroides* – Larger Mouse-tail Moss (Rampant Happiness) and *Brachythecium rutabulum* – Rough-stalked Feather-moss (Home Fires) – I say their names now that I know them. I bend my ear low. It is not the wind but the sun that they sing of – its spread through their body, slow and rich, in a steady drip:

> Moss, the greenest of the doves,
> Lights and leads you back with love.

As I retrace my steps down the valley, tiny dawns breaking underfoot, the words of the Irish song, 'The Streams of Bunclody', begin to surface. Opening with the lament: 'Oh were I at the Moss House, where the birds do increase / At the foot of Mount Leinster or some silent place' (ll. 1–2), in Séamas S. de Vál's 'Some Versions of "The Streams of Bunclody"' from Colm Ó Lochlainn's *Irish Street Ballads*,[19] the song presents a scenario that strikes a chord for many who have grown up close to the land but have since had to leave. The speaker reveals how 'Once I lived in Bunclody but now must remove' (l. 16), when faced with a situation where his love 'has got a freehold and I have no land' (l. 22). It is the story of my father's family in this very valley. It is the story, too, of my mother and of her mother.

When their village was attacked, suspected of harbouring members of the Mau Mau, they were forced to move in the dead of the night, with the house set alight. When the storm blazed and the buildings burned, each one gave itself over to the flames. And the flash of the dark, beating, grew in my mother and her mother, became a part of them they leaned into, without turning away. But I do not need to enter the flames to feel their undoing. To know how the force of this history would shred me like a leopard and I would limp away, without looking. The human skin of me. The mess that skin can make of stories, in its halfway house between telling and re-telling.

Still, we are miraculous. Time moves off us like wax. In the fold of the dark, we mutter and part our lips with the drip of the past pouring in. Still, we persist. When I listen to her story, of people moved not by deeds or a transfer of money but a blade and a whip and a flurry of flames, I do not ignite in the dark with leaf-light, but muffle with years, the fear of it. I am the moss that came after the fire. In the space that emerges after catastrophic disturbance, mosses will thrive. I say things to my mother like *sigh*. Like saliva, which sounds, in its rustle of breath, like, *survivor*. And so we lean in, the two of us, not all at once, with the openness of mosses but with little shuffles of trust. Little shakes of the head and stretches of skin. Small ways of saying, *Come in*. Then, when I wonder where to begin to let my own sound in, I think of the song thrush who sings in the night and the mosses who sing of the light and find myself caught somewhere in between.

At the foot of the valley, I lie against an oak clothed in Marilyn. There are very little sounds – of leaf tips and eyelids, stretches of stem, small rustles and shuffles of muscle. There are huge sounds – of wide winds borne of high seas, not used to stopping. They hurl into the mosses with the force of those not used to opposition. But

it is no use being angry at a moss. They only know soft. You can
storm and you can seethe but they will warm and they will ease.

If touched they will warm
if blushed they will form
a circuit of light in the bark
to lead you with leaves
in shimmering wreaths
small halos that burn in the dark.
In the rush of the ground letting go
all that's buried inside of its loam
there are altars of light where the old mosses glow.

11. CHAMPAGNE

BIRMINGHAM

There are altars of light where the old mosses glow, inside the body
what was buried will grow. For, after a period of planting joy into
darkness, the time will come for harvest. And there will be no use,
then, beating it back with a stick, saying 'Down, joy, down', as
the damage will already have been done. Try holding a halo inside
you. It will stretch through the skin and win through, everyone will
see it, whatever you do. If touched it will warm, if blushed it will
form a circuit of light you can't hide. Still, you may try to conceal
it. Because somewhere along the way we learn that it is safer to
keep valuables hidden. So, fear comes and helps to heap over the
earth, muffling music with the thud of its sod. But you have not
done all this planting to be defeated by the first failed crop. Again,
and again, joy batters the body. It will be heard. It will be seen. It
will not be confined to dream.

For a year, the mosses I had gathered from Cave Valley had
lived in my room; beside me when I worked, when I wrote, when
I planned, when I hoped. I had watered them, spoken to them,
sometimes stroked and sometimes forgotten them. I had lined my
shoes with them – the boundary layer between foot and sole, skin
and stone – and they had travelled with me, making little temporary homes. Each time I had needed to go where I didn't want
to go, the mosses had come with me and said, *Glow*. Each time I
hadn't felt like being seen, the mosses had said, *Be like Marilyn*.
Each time I had lain weakened by fears, the mosses said, *Charge
on with Kind Spears*. A tight, inner-city office can become a forest
with the mosses – a way of belonging when displaced, the living
lights in a dark place.

But the mosses wilted. Away from their homeland, though
watered, they grew tired. Though heated, they lacked fire. Over

the months, my moss shoes lost their linings, left with only thin pinings for what these plants used to be. Left shoe: one branch of Marilyn; right shoe: one of Kind Spears. The rest, matted together in mossy protest, made it clear that they had done enough to help. If I had plans to move, then so did they and theirs would not take any further delay.

I pick myself up. No longer waiting for another to move me along, today, the motion is mine – I have listened and now is the time. Even mosses, with their ability to grow in the tightest of spots and not rot in the places the sun forgot – even mosses who forge life from almost nothing, weathering flooding – even mosses have places they prefer to be, with positions that enable their brightest green. The picture that had started to form when I had softened, as a peaceful warrior dropping her barriers, is here. It took a long time to give happiness permission and even longer for joy to grow unbidden. But once it had begun, there was no going back. Or, rather, there is nothing but going back.

CAVE VALLEY

Out from the rock's crack, further and further, the body is a flying tide. Closer and closer – little, winged mouse. Then, two. Then, three. All flying towards me. I wonder where they can be when they retreat into a distance I cannot see, into layers impenetrable to me – what kind of life they lead there, before releasing with a screech that sears like a sabre, into daylight. A cave is the place to visit when you are empty. You can stand for hours by its mouth saying, *That looks like me.* You can call into its spout and hear yourself repeat. You can watch and wait for something to happen, anything. So, when a bat screeches out with a friendly, flapping fury, that is something happening. When a life lived long in darkness forays into day with such sparkiness, that is something happening. The heart is a bat. Watch, how it leaps into light.

Place your hand over your bat and wait for the flap of its wings. Begin. Pour all your weight into one foot. Hop. Use every available toe, heel, ball. Swap. On your other foot, trot. Clip-clop. From your waist now, turning. Body learning from the trickle-up effect of your fleet feet. Your swinging torso ending in fingers extending, tendrils, testing, twisting, little mossy bio-indicators: how is the air affecting me? There is a discipline to it. You will want to stop, to let one foot follow the other as it has always done.

Persist. Continue what is good for you as long as it is good for you. Sheep may stare. But it is good, now and then, to astound a sheep. Snowdrops leap out of hedgerows, blowing white kisses as you hop, skip, fall, lift, and the bat says that this is what it misses. When you keep it too long in its cave, in familiar shape, it will try to escape to be kissed by snow, to shift and flow into possibility. You are either with it, or against it. You can swat it back into flatness, watch it weaken into seizure, or let it release with a high, thin screech into slits of shape that were overlooked but were all it took to begin again; breath and again breath, over and among the thronging mosses, low and deep, the crawl and creep of the honest – of the sound you make when the shape you take is a promise to your battered, bat-hearted body and all who fly with it, to permit no limits to its soar.

I press the mosses back into the boulders they had come from and bring my mouth to the cave's. A dank smell rots out from the edges, pushing me back. In this drawn-out age of extractive industry, the traces of discontinued mining are still prominent, even as they slide under larger projects by global conglomerates. Metals layer over coal, as Devon, Europe and Africa map onto every continent except Antarctica. Then, where is the bat heart in this and how ever might joy persist? While the scale of extraction must change, there are signs of the potential to save; where damaged earth is now a home for bats, where the mosses teem, once more intact. And so the cave tells me to go back, out into the greening rain, out, into the world again, and, as I open my mouth, what I think will be a primal release of stress, by the time it reaches air, is something else. The softness from the mosses rebounds. I only want to make loving sounds.

What the mosses say in the dark, I tell in the light. In the deep recesses, not often visited, set apart from the outside world, what they say is in the drop of water off the cool cave walls, in the powdered lichen on the sprawling rock, in the long unfolding of the growing moss that speaks of slowness and a thriving loss. They cover a land blown apart by mines and mother a thigh-bone bleached clean by time. However deep the chasm, they don't leave you alone – theirs is the comfort that builds you a home, even in the wilderness – wasteland – wetland, they trickle through the letters we grow for the land.

RIVER DOVE

I cross over the ground between M and me, arriving on Words-worth's birthday in new surroundings. A small patch of lawn leads to a garage, which M's neighbours periodically pop in and out of, with low fences dividing the gardens on both sides. As people enjoy the little space they have through the course of the day, I consider stretching branches from left to right, fence to fence, rising to one high dome, mosses layered in between. Scaled down, I think of moss-papering the kitchen.

But inside, I know that even the smallest of constructions will be too much for me. I still feel the agony of my moss shoes – of taking any amount of these plants from where they are growing for my own benefit. I cannot bear it. Instead, I think of the moss huts that springtails may build by scurrying among the leafy mounds. Could I, perhaps, visit one of them?

At midday, the spring sun is strong. Mosses like a little shade, so I've brought a parasol fashioned from a cocktail stick and a sheet of toilet paper. I've brought one spray-can filled with water, one with champagne, and, as I approach, find that I have butter-flies. Just as with a party where you won't know anyone, I am nervous about who I'll meet and what they'll make of me. As M sets his telescope up to watch for waders, I sit by a bank of Kind Spears and Marilyn.

After the necessary introductions have been made, I start to take a proper look at my hosts and find that the party is already underway. Tapering sporophytes, like stems of wine glasses, are flushed with amber in the clinking capsule heads. Eager to bring them libations, I find them already replete. It is hard to tell where the well-meaning wish to establish a connection starts and assumptions about their needing something I might be able to offer take over. After some time baking in the sunlight, I mist the mosses. With water and champagne, we toast Wordsworth's birthday.

The days move fast with M. We fling and flow in a rushing confluence. Moving through the fields, I gather my inventories: Kind Spears, Marilyn, cow parsley; cowslip, euphorbia, daisy; hawthorn, forget-me-not, yellow archangel; rose, red campion, white dead-nettle. M's focus is a higher prowl: waders, yellowhammers, little owls.

We watch, tonight, for the flower moon but it is the sun and the sun and the sun that refuses to ever leave the tops of the fields, never to sink or to peel away to moonlight. On and on the night goes but the sun carries on as though it doesn't know anyone is waiting – that a moon will need placating. And just when we glimpse the tip of the night, the clouds throw open another slice of light, a haze of orange and purple and pink, a light so slow, it stalls on the brink of the treetops. There is no taking our eyes off it. Every angle is better than the last, every moment seems like it will never pass. Until, the final, triumphant flare as colour falls away from air, leaving nothing to do but stare.

The next day, the sun echoes everywhere. Yellow in the ears with the yellowhammers. Yellow in the fields with the rapeseed. Yellow up-close in the buttercup. Yellow far off in the oak leaves. At our

feet, Marilyn moss – lemon and white – and yellow archangel net-
tles billowing bright and the upward note of a lapwing from the
river, bringing a shiver of song to the grass as I ask: what is the word
for the start of joy? For it doesn't always move directly – boom –
from sadness to joy – you sometimes need to lay the groundwork
for it to begin. So, what is the word for this first fuzz? The first push
through earth? Is there a word that describes the way yellow can rise
from a moss to a nettle, from an oak to a bird, until, all at once, it is
the only colour to be heard and the air starts to heave with the yel-
lowhammer's song, 'A little bit of bread and no cheese!'

In this new place with M, fresh light brimming over the soil, I
look for a vocabulary for joy – not the full-blown flood of it but
the slow increments that start it. I search for words that might
bubble and gather – upwards, in a scale – then clamour, from a
whisper to a full happiness gale. And I find them. For one moment,
bind them.

| burst |

| out |

| goldfinch | slow inch | stretch | out |

| worn path | whitethroat | fresh heart | lit grass |

| red campion | white dead-nettle | sun that slows |

| shiver of song | grass | bluebell | rose |

| marilyn moss | archangel nettle | lapwing note |

| yellowhammer | rapeseed | buttercup | oak

Yet, even through the high top notes, I sense the lower undertones. Without the familiarity of my old home, I see the bottom of the riverbed. Something moves in the sediment. Frequently moved on by others – a bird gathering material for a nest, or raindrop carrying a spore – mosses have the ability to make a life where they are thrown. There are even mobile mounds of mosses, a phenomenon the Icelandic researcher Jon Eythorsson called '*jökla-mýs*' or 'glacier mice', as he marvelled in an article of the same name in the *Journal of Glaciology*, that 'rolling stones *can* gather moss'.[20] These glacier mice moving small distances over ground – plants that can pick themselves up and set themselves back down without harm – have a dexterous approach to home-making. But for humans, moving is not always seamless.

A blackbird swoops past with a beakful of moss – Glowflake, Kind Spears and Marilyn mixed. Others flit amid the blackthorn, busy building with mosses and other softnesses: a catkin, a pigeon's feather, a little tuft of fur. In this field filled with young mothers, I feel unsure who to follow. The thrush who brings her body back and forth, back and forth, from ground to nest, scoping for worms in the soil, pausing to scout for intruders on the bush, before making her dash to the nest. The blackbird who, surprised by the arrival of her offspring, calls from makeshift twigs, cobbled together last-minute by a frantic partner. The unknown mother who deposited her egg inside a rotting log. They fill the air with their pressing need.

But it is hard to make a nest in the middle of your life. When you have already seen so many and watched them pass, when there has not seemed a way to make them last. I watch the word nest, where it lies hidden in the word *honest*. As I build a new nest now it must be that and more, an *earnest* one – that you can put your ear to – a place where you can listen and be listened to.

M joins me on the bank as we watch an egret lift. Even midway in life, what is fixed can be unfixed, what is anchored set adrift. So, perhaps, it is not the blackbird who goes around and around with its twig in its mouth that makes the best guide, but Penelope, undoing her stitches at night. In the tale of *The Odyssey*, Odysseus' wife, Penelope, waits faithfully for his return from the Trojan War. In order to put off suitors, she agrees to marry once she's finished weaving a burial shroud for his father, only to secretly undo each day's stitching. Penelope: the unmaker of nests.

Today, the name Penelope is connected to the wigeon through the Linnaean binomial, *Anas penelope*. It is one of M's favourite birds. He talks about how they love the floodwater. How they writhe together in flocks. How a nearby hill we have climbed rises over ground that floods in winter, where hundreds of them gather. *Birds of a feather*, I think, watching his face light at the thought. I flush in bright rapport.

As we settle by the confluence where the rivers Trent and Dove meet, I recall one of Wordsworth's Lucy poems, 'Song', where he writes of a love who 'dwelt among th' untrodden ways / Beside the springs of Dove' (ll. 1–2).[21] Love and moss almost come together in this poem which draws light on 'A violet by a mossy stone' that is 'Half-hidden from the eye!' Yet, it is the violet, rather than the moss that is pulled into focus, as the moss beside the violet remains overlooked. Wordsworth had, though, valued the plant enough to want to encase his own life in a mossy architecture, having a moss hut built in his Grasmere garden. Inspired by rustic 'fog houses' in Scotland, the Wordsworths built their soft nook, to gather their writing, dreaming and books. Wordsworth himself, perhaps, described it best, in a letter to Sir George Beaumont, 25 December 1804, as a 'little circular hut lined with moss like a wren's nest'.[22]

My moss neighbours have always brought comfort when I have drifted and I want to repay their assistance. But, when I think of the toilet-paper parasol I had made for them, it doesn't seem to measure up as a return gift. If I am to really repay them for their sculpted company – the Grasmere moss hut for the Wordsworths, the Cave Valley shoes for me – I would need to cover them in a human hut – to fold my body into protective contortions. Even then, I'm doubtful as to whether my skin could be as welcome to them as their leaves are to me. Yet, the high notes of joy won't give such reservations a chance – joy will say, *Let's take a look, let's advance!*

So, with a barrier of hawthorn and blackcaps obscuring me from M, I try out some basic human hut structures. Bending backwards, torso raised like a bridge; bending forwards, back arched like a cat. But I am impossibly large. I try again using a finger. Bent at the knuckle, moss underneath; bent at the tip, moss sheathed by skin. I look in. The mosses are doing something like sleeping. Nestled in fur, dew on their tips like milk delivered and left on the step – not required yet. I roll down the sleeve of my cardigan and tuck them in. The air touches and the mite and the worm turn. Toward each motion, my body curves. Curled on the hill, charging with light, I wait with the moss for the next patch of life.

12. GOLDRUSH

THE CINDER PATH

I stand in the moss in the flood of the light. The daisies are up. The Sweet Williams are up. Every colour is up except green. Green is still filling in – it needs the whole of the sun to be fully itself. Light on the tops of the ivy, light from the gap in the hedge, light from the next field pouring over the waxy stretch of the holly. Huge bursts of light upon the docks. Light through and over the dots of mature trees framing the land and the sky. Light in the foreground, on the dog rose – leaving it resplendent, full-white. Its fallen hearts flower the floor, trailing a layered softness where I walk.

On the Cinder Path that goes out before coming back around and with the mosses returned to their earlier ground, there is strength in a circle forming, there is joy in the act of turning. The earth, which is never the same distance from the sun, knows it is not the scale of the turn that is important, only its persistence. And, though I may not, always, leap like a springtail from sadness' presence, I know, now, how to turn a cheek – to get out of the way and let the body speak. So that, sometimes, the turn away is small – a tiny increment of leaning – and sometimes it is a wide swell of meaning. Cycles of light and season move me back and forth between them.

Days pass. On this visit to my mother, I find myself often looking up. Now the sky is sand – vast golden stretches, deserts of light. 'The leopard has given birth,' Mum says, looking at the clouds – a Kikuyu phrase for when puffball clouds seem to clothe the sky in a kind of leopard print. I think of the words we had once drawn together for moss. '*Makundi kindogo ya*' – clouds – '*wanaishi pamoja!*' I say. A group of small – clouds – growing together! She laughs and supplies the missing word – '*mawingu*' – so the mosses underfoot and the clouds overhead, and the animal sky and the vegetable bed, and my mother's history and our present together, a nest she has left and the one we now feather, the man we both lost but who'll never be left and the joy that returns and the sadness that ebbs are joined – for a moment, tethered.

The light goes on and on, in these solstice days, refusing to give way to the night, which, when it comes, is a blanket placed around a child who won't sleep, who wants to go on, never tiring. The moon slips. The bat flits. The spider hangs. The rose won't let go of its colour. I sleep in short bursts. There is too much light to fall into dark. Mist comes. Swathes of incoming grey. At four o'clock, the sky is already flushed blue. The rose has held its colour. The bat has gone and the moon is not long behind. The spider has spun away.

I pull another layer on, in the turn of night to day. I know what it is to be a body within a body, a Russian doll – *babushka* – a fold within a fold of selves. My English grandmother moving from Devon hill to Devon hill, my Kenyan *bibi* moving across a mountain foothill. One soft move, one violent. Both flicker inside and it seems only right that I should feel their flare, here with my mother and the land that we share. I have travelled to many wetlands in the time since my father passed but the one in a mother's body held me first and calls me last.

Days pass. I know the early-morning strains of one thrush so well. The same bursts of repeated notes, distinct phrases in succession. Like an oral poetry, the thrush passes on a history, tells its bracing story of thrushness. I think of the farmers, too, up at this hour, and my farming family's circadian rhythms, so often set to the time of the fields. The farmer's gun. A scatter of crows from the hay. Mist on the cabbages lands with the look of frost. Sweetness from the hay as its scent pours off and rolls in from the far field giving depth to the air, hanging, just floating there, in the treacled grass.

The scent of the hay gives over to moss, a deep earthiness and dock, pine needles. And the lime Marilyn lies among the self-heal and the clover and the cobwebs line the grass where I kneel. Low on the ground, the prominence of the birds recedes as the moss carpet gleams. The feathery Glowflake and deep mats of Kind Spears rush together in a golden stream.

GOLDRUSH
Glowflake, Kind Spears and Marilyn

All through the dark seasons, the low, hot lick
of arteries threading their ruffled pinks
goes unnoticed; only when a cool
stone is placed upon the tongue, only
when the moon foams back and forth between
the lungs, only when all the light has poured
into the mould of your risen body
does it stop – you have dug enough.

The air is still so warm as I pull up at the top of the field I have grown with. The cows are asleep where the mist gathers in the crook of the valley and over the darkness is a pink. And over the pink is a peach. Dots of sheep. Then, the high, red glow of the hill – my panorama through the decades, unaltered still. A world waking. A calm. Scent of pea and lemon balm.

And the sawing note of the greenfinch meets the soaring coat of the moss – lifts its green up. A blackbird chorus rises from the copse – one in the high oak, one in the beech, one in the willow and one in the deep rummage of the hedge. And the pigeons coo and the blackbirds yap as I trace small orbs of white – tangled, the dog rose crawls along the bramble. Then the Glowflakes shine their little lemon lights and trails of Kind Spears and Glowflake are bundled up tight and I think of the singing that comes after the night. How silence and sounding can join in a song and a ritual process of singing might even bring lost species back into being. Let us try it and sing of the mosses. Let our song be porous, as we join in its chorus.

In a rhythm that is bound to the moss, I feel my way without sinking – a Sphagnum, partly dead yet still drinking in sun. Wherever there is light I gratefully choose it and where there is moss there will always be music. For moss is the light of the earth and when it grows inside it cannot be hidden but courses through the limp stitching of the body. You may have closed yourself off and been bound up tight, hovering unbearably on the brink of the night, yet, do not lose heart. There is growing in you a family of light, scattered, yet connected, a symphony of brightness plays its ghost-notes through the blood you thought you had lost – that is moss, growing on your gleaming bones, threading the song of you into the stones, flooding the spires of your tapering homes – that is moss and not loss that shapes you.

Days pass. Silence in the hedgerows, the beating bodies stilled. In the grass, blankets of broken branch. Orbs of leaf. Sun flashes over bark, grass, heart – reminds us of the parts that we have filled. Then, stumbles in the bushes. Stutters of feathers. Claws on twig.

Sound moves fast, overdue. And into the clumps of the mosses the sun slips, into their cups and lathers their leaves. And it is the song thrush first – that repeated refrain, that blowing of a whistle, again and again – breaking our reverie with its bravery. We remember stars. We remember luminosity. We remember our bodies are made for more than weathering. An insect bites and a snail trails. A door opens and a spade falls. A cabbage is cut and beaten and thrown down. A dog rose lifts and ripples with the sun. The moon is a slit of fire in wide blue, blackbird and robin and pigeon call through and all of us seem to know the tune. In every cell the light repeats. I hear the ripeness in the leaves. Something endless runs through me. The air is pressed with melody.

Acknowledgements

As mosses grow in groups, so books are made collectively. I would like to thank my editor, Josephine Greywoode, and agent, Cathryn Summerhayes. Special thanks to my mother, Polly: *nuru mng'aro yangu*. Thanks also to my friends Louise, Camilla and M and to my interviewees: Margaret Anderson, Alys Fowler, Trish Fox, Deborah Land and Olly Watts, the bryologist Lucia Ruffino and my niece, Louisa. Thank you to the British Academy for a small grant (2018–21) funding some early fieldwork and consultation and to the Leverhulme Trust for a Leverhulme Research Fellowship (2021–22) that allowed me to extend the scope of the book. Thanks to Harriet Tarlo, Richard Kerridge and Jonathan Skinner and to the publishers and venues who engaged with the poems. 'Little Peach' featured in the *Willowherb Review*, 2019 and at the Serpentine Gallery in *The Shape of a Circle in the Mind of a Fish: The Understory of the Understory*, December 2020; 'Marilyn' was a part of the Timepiece Collective at *Climate Week NYC*, 21 September 2020; and 'Glowflake' featured in 'Green Memoir' on Radio 3's *The Verb*, 13 November 2020. Thank you to the community at Sheldon, to David and all the mosses encountered, particularly those from my 'moss shoes'.

Notes

1 Alys Fowler, *Hidden Nature* (Hodder & Stoughton, 2017), p. 14.

2 Ron Porley and Nick Hodgetts, *Mosses and Liverworts* (Collins, 2005), p. xi.

3 Robert Graves, *The White Goddess: A Historical Grammar of Poetic Myth* (Faber & Faber, 1961), p. 19.

4 Felicia Hemans, *The Poetical Works of Felicia Dorothea Hemans* (Oxford University Press, 1914), pp. 176–7.

5 P. G. Kareru, G. M. Kenji, A. N. Gachanja, J. M. Keriko, G. Mungai, 'Traditional Medicines among the Embu and Mbeere Peoples of Kenya', *African Journal of Traditional, Complementary and Alternative Medicines*, 2007; 4.1, p. 76. Published online 28 August 2006, doi: <10.4314/ajtcam.v4i1.31193>, at https://www.ncbi.nlm.nih.gov/pmc/articles/PMC2816425/; accessed 10 November 2021.

6 Robin Kimmerer, *Gathering Moss* (Oregon State University, 2003), p. 85.

7 W. B. Yeats, 'The Wild Swans at Coole', in Timothy Webb (ed.), *W. B. Yeats: Selected Poems* (Penguin, 2000), p. 85.

8 Emily Brontë, *Wuthering Heights* (Penguin Books, 2003), pp. 85 and 335.

9 Brontë, *Wuthering Heights* (2003), p. 337.

10 John Clare, 'To the Snipe', in Eric Robinson, David Powell, P. M. S. Dawson (eds.), *Poems of the Middle Period, 1822–1837*, (Clarendon Press, 1998), pp. 576–7.

11 Audre Lorde, 'Poetry Is Not a Luxury', *Sister Outsider: Essays and Speeches* (Crossing Press, 2007), p. 37.

12 'The Whiteman is by Thagana River', recorded and translated by H. S. K. Mwaniki in *Categories and Substance of Embu Traditional Songs and Dances* (Kenya Literature Bureau, 1986), p. 23.

13 'Beowulf' in Bruce Mitchell and Fred C. Robinson (eds.), *A Guide to Old English*, fifth edn (Blackwell Publishers Ltd, 1996), pp. 288–9.

14 Michael Alexander (ed.), *Beowulf: A Glossed Text* (Penguin, 2005), p. 56.

15 'I Syng of a Mayden', *English Medieval Religious Lyrics*, ed. Douglas Gray (Liverpool University Press, 1992), pp. 4–5.

16 Jackson J. Campbell (ed.), *Advent Lyrics of the Exeter Book* (Princeton University Press, 1959), p. 48.

17 John Audelay, 'There Is a Flower', in E. K. Chambers and F. Sidgwick (eds.), *Early English Lyrics* (A. H. Bullen, 1907), pp. 110–11.

18 Audre Lorde, 'The Transformation of Silence into Language and Action', *Sister Outsider: Essays and Speeches* (Crossing Press, 2007), p. 41.

19 Séamas S. de Vál, 'Some Versions of "The Streams of Bunclody"', *The Past: The Organ of the Uí Cinsealaigh Historical Society*, Uí Cinsealaigh Historical Society, 29, 2008, pp. 90–95. The lines of the songs are quoted from Colm Ó Lochlainn's *Irish Street Ballads* (1939).

20 Jon Eythorsson, 'Jökla-mýs', *Journal of Glaciology*, Vol. 1, no. 9, 1951, p. 503.

21 William Wordsworth, 'Song', in *William Wordsworth*, ed. Stephen Gill (Oxford University Press, 1990), p. 147.

22 William Wordsworth, letter to Sir George Beaumont, 25 December 1804, in Lucy Newlyn, *William and Dorothy Wordsworth: All in Each Other* (Oxford University Press, 2013), p. 210.